CW00431801

EMPIRES OF NATURE AND
THE NATURE OF EMPIRES

EMPIRES OF NATURE AND THE NATURE OF EMPIRES

Imperialism, Scotland and the Environment

*The Callander Lectures
delivered in the University of Aberdeen,
2–7 November 1995*

*by
John M. MacKenzie*

TUCKWELL PRESS

First published in 1997 in Great Britain by
Tuckwell Press Ltd
The Mill House
Phantassie
East Linton East Lothian EH40 3DG

ISBN 1 86232 059 4

British Library Cataloguing-in-Publication Data
A catalogue record for this book is available
on request from the British Library

Typeset by Carnegie Publishing, 18 Maynard St, Preston
Printed and bound by
Cromwell Press, Broughton Gifford, Melksham, Wiltshire

Contents

Foreword

THE Callander Lectures in the University of Aberdeen com-
memorate the life and interests of one of its graduates,
Professor Thomas Callander. The first series of lectures was delivered by Professor Owen Lattimore in 1973 under the general
title of 'Empire and Revolution'. This followed over three years
of negotiations on the best means by which the University could
utilise a generous bequest from the Callander family to promote
thinking and discussion on some key issues of twentieth-century
history which had been of great concern to Thomas Callander
himself. The initiative was taken in 1969 by his niece, Miss
E. G. Whitelaw, when it became apparent that a sum of money
could be made available to the University by the Trustees of
Professor and Mrs Callander following the death of Mrs Callander
in 1968. Acting for the University, Professor John Hargreaves was
principally responsible for devising academic proposals which were
acceptable to the Trustees. The University and the wider academic
community owe a debt of gratitude to Miss Whitelaw and to
Professor Hargreaves for producing the arrangements which have
led to the delivery of ten series of lectures under the general
heading of 'War and Empire in the Twentieth Century' by a
succession of highly distinguished lecturers. Their contributions
have certainly generated an interest and concern which would
surely have gratified Professor Callander.

Thomas Callander lived from 1877 to 1959. He became a
classical scholar and graduated from the University of Aberdeen
in 1898. From 1904 until 1934, he held the Chair of Greek in

Queen's University at Kingston, Ontario where he became a well-known figure to several generations of students. It seems that, perhaps partly as a result of living in what was still part of the British Empire, his studies of the Peloponnesian War and other developments in the rise of the Athenian Empire led him to look with an increasingly critical eye at events in international politics as they unfolded in his own lifetime. In particular, he began to see imperialism, and British imperialism in particular, as being not a noble cause but a phenomenon which led to war and misery. Not only were there mistaken assumptions about political imperatives but also, and more seriously, moral failings by the politicians and statesmen who were promoting imperialist policies. The Great War, the injustices of the Treaty of Versailles and, later, the Second World War were the consequences. These ideas were set out at some length in his posthumously-published work, *The Athenian Empire and the British* (Weidenfeld, 1961). Following his retirement to the Channel Islands, Callander had suffered internment by the Germans during the Second World War but his personal life was consistent with his scholarly position on the failings of extreme nationalism: he refused to hate all Germans and had resumed contacts with fellow scholars in that country as soon as possible in 1945. His widow was no doubt reflecting their ideals when making it clear that she wished her trustees to find ways of encouraging thought and debate on the issues which had so much exercised Professor Callander.

Clearly, it would have been ultimately stultifying to have concentrated narrowly in the lecture series on the precise political issues which so concerned Thomas Callander; the world has moved on and so has academic research and debate on the nature of modern imperialism. Hence the University's Callander Lectures Committee has sought to fulfil the wishes of Professor Callander and his trustees by engaging the services of speakers who, either by their academic publications or by their engagement with the practical problems of Empire, have widened and deepened our understanding of this most important feature of the modern world.

Owen Lattimore's lectures were concerned mainly with the Chinese Empire and its fate at the hands of modern imperialism. In 1975, Lord Caradon reflected on his own involvement in the decolonisation process and the emergence of new powers in the United Nations. Sir Michael Howard in 1978 discussed the development of war and imperialism in the period just after Callander had taken up his chair. Then Kenneth Robinson gave a scholarly account of the work of the Colonial Office as Britain's African empire moved towards self-government. In 1981, there were two sets of lectures: William Kirk considered imperial frontiers, especially in modern India, whilst Sir Shridath Ramphal reflected on the character of the post-imperial world and on the problems with which he had to deal as Secretary-General of the Commonwealth. In the following year, Immanuel Geiss provided a remarkable analysis of empires and the genesis of wars in the twentieth century. Ali Mazrui, lecturing in 1984, took an African perspective on the transition from British to American hegemony, and three years later Walter La Feber took as his subject the rise of the empires of the super-powers from 1900. All of these lecture subjects figured in publications of some kind, in two cases these being direct publications of the texts.[1]

The Callander Lectures Committee believes that the policy of publication should become the normal procedure, even at the cost of rather less frequent lecture series. Hence the present work. The Committee was also willing to agree, however, that the Callander Lectures ought to be delivered during the period of the University of Aberdeen's Quincentenary celebrations as one of the signs that, after five hundred years, the University remained determined to promote scholarship of the highest order. We were fortunate indeed that Professor John MacKenzie was willing to become the Callander Lecturer in November 1995, for no-one has done more in recent years to establish new approaches to the study of imperialism.

A Scot educated in Zambia and Canada as well as Glasgow, John MacKenzie seems uniquely well endowed to study empire

which he has done not only in those countries but in Southern
and Eastern Africa and in India. His publications include *Propaganda
and Empire; Imperialism and Popular Culture* (editor); *Popular Imperialism and the Military* (editor) and, recently, *Orientalism: History,
Theory and the Arts,* all these works showing his mastery of the
cultural, political and military aspects of imperialism. But it was
with the book entitled *The Empire of Nature* in 1988 and then his
edited collection two years later, *Imperialism and the Natural World,*
that John MacKenzie attracted attention far beyond the confines
of academic history by showing that imperialism and what it
entails must be seen as a major factor in environmental, botanical
and zoological developments in the modern world.

The University of Aberdeen is pleased to have been able to
provide Professor MacKenzie with the opportunity to develop
and extend some of his ideas and, not least, to show how Scotland
has been involved in the processes he describes so lucidly and
entertainingly. I would like to extend my personal thanks to John
MacKenzie himself for agreeing to lecture and for co-operating
patiently in the preparation of this publication. I would also
acknowledge the help and advice of two successive Vice-Principals
and Deans of the Faculty of Arts and Divinity, also Conveners
of the Callander Committee, Professor Ian Macdonald and Dr
Graeme Roberts. Finally, I warmly acknowledge the interest
shown and the kind hospitality extended in 1995 by the then
Principal of the University of Aberdeen, Professor J. Maxwell
Irvine.

Roy Bridges
Professor of History

December 1996

NOTE

1. Shridath S. Ramphal, *Sovereignty or Solidarity,* Aberdeen, n.d.;
   Immanuel Geiss, *War and Empire in the Twentieth Century*, Aberdeen,
   1983.

Introduction

NINETEEN NINETY-FIVE was an auspicious year in which to deliver the Callander Lectures. Not only was it the quincentennial of the founding of the University of Aberdeen, it was also the year when environmental history seemed to come of age. Many new works demonstrated the remarkable vigour of studies in the field as well as its highly creative multi-disciplinary character. This is illustrated by a new and rapidly flourishing journal, *Environment and History*,[1] which first appeared in this year. Simon Schama published his *Landscape and Memory*, a dense, post-modernist and very personal work in which he explored the cultural construction of aspects of the natural world within a European nationalist framework.[2] Richard Grove's long-awaited *Green Imperialism* also appeared in 1995, controversially asserting the contribution of European imperialism, particularly in tropical oceanic islands, to the development of environmental ideas.[3] And a collection of papers, *Nature, Culture, Imperialism: Essays on the Environmental History of South Asia*, edited by David Arnold and Ramachandra Guha, revealed the importance and sophistication of the environmental history being written in and about South Asia.[4]

Some of these studies, fresh from the press, were available to me when I came to write the Callander Lectures in the autumn of 1995. Others came out soon afterwards and yet more have only recently come to hand. Perhaps the most striking characteristic of this 'new' environmental history is the manner in which ecological issues are being placed in their cultural, anthropological and political, as well as economic, contexts. This is amply demonstrated by three new books from imperial settler territories, the old 'dominions'. Jane Carruthers' history of the Kruger National Park explores the significance of this celebrated park to Afrikaner nationalism and white national identity as well as to the African people and their ecology in which it was founded.[5] Geoff Park's *Nga Uruora* ('the groves of life' in the Maori language) brings together a personal and romantic experience of landscape with a sustained analysis of the Maori and Pakeha (white) approaches to exploitation, degradation and sustainability in the fertile coastal plains of both North and South Islands.[6] It also explores the responses of art and photography to these lands, where survival, economics, and spirituality profoundly intermingle. Tom Griffiths' *Hunters and Collectors* shifts the focus to the development of the antiquarian imagination in Australia and the hunting and collecting activities that took place within a landscape that was being repeatedly re-evaluated by settlers, even as their relationship with both Aborigines, geological and human time-scales, and their own ancestors was progressively transformed.[7]

Such richness and diversity help to justify, if justification were necessary, the need for historiographical and comparative studies of these new ways of thinking about human interactions with their ecological contexts. In an article, published in 1996, too late to be used in these lectures, Mahesh Rangarajan argued for just such an approach: the diversity and rich human histories of South Asia ensured that its environmental history had much to offer practitioners elsewhere.[8] Analysis of its various modes was a necessary prerequisite to this. Nevertheless, historians of the Indian natural world had to break free of the notion that their history was only about degradation and decline and the identification of heroes and villains in the ecological past.

Rangarajan was in effect arguing that such studies should transcend their national, regional or continental locations and escape from their rather blinkered moralising tendencies. The question that arises is the extent to which the history of the British Empire (and other European empires) helps with this process or merely throws a much larger, and equally disabling, frame over the analysis. Current evidence does seem to offer a positive answer; imperial environmental history, however freely interpreted, has helped the process of globalising environmental studies. Despite the vast complexities of the imperial condition, common political, legal, military, and economic cultures do suggest fruitful comparative analyses. Historians of Africa, India, the Pacific and Australasia can indeed find common ground. Global models, which have been dominated by economic historians in the past, may yet emerge from such cross-fertilisation.

The modern study of the natural environment and its reciprocal influence on human history has often been dated to the early 1970s. American scholars have ascribed this development to the emergence of the American green movement in those years and have suggested that it consequently had a strongly moral impulse. They have also tended to emphasise the role of historians of the United States in this new development. In 1995 Alfred Crosby (himself no mean globaliser) re-emphasised this in his article 'The Past and Present of Environmental History'.[9] Donald Worster has paradoxically seen environmental history as superseding the nationalist history of the late nineteenth and early twentieth centuries, but has then provided a strongly American nationalist slant to the development of the new discipline.[10]

But this view has been spiritedly contested by Richard Grove, both in *Green Imperialism* and in an unpublished paper he delivered at the Australian National University in early 1996.[11] He traces environmental ideas arising out of the European contact with the wider world to at least the late seventeenth century. Moreover, while the development of the modern environmental history of empire can also be traced to the early 1970s, its origins can be found further back in the work of physical geographers and natural scientists associated with empire.

Such debates, though apparently sterile on the surface, do stimulate the unveiling and reinterpretation of the work of the past, providing perspective and context to modern studies. My own African antecedents include a boyhood in Zambia and primary research in Zimbabwe in the late 1960s and early 1970s. A number of examples occur to me from this region. Archaeologists and anthropologists have been dealing in key environmental issues for many years. For example, discussion of the ebb and flow of tsetse belts in East and Central Africa, connected with climatic change, vegetation cover, rainfall and temperature, has been a commonplace in the study of migration and settlement in the region since at least the 1960s. The pioneering work of Audrey Richards in Zambia in the 1930s revealed the relationship of agricultural methods in specific environmental contexts with human diet and nutrition.[12] The widespread fascination with natural history in the late nineteenth and early twentieth centuries, not least in the study of animals and their habitats, increased awareness of historic environmental change. And thus the trail can be taken yet further back.

The new environmental history builds on this richly productive background while driving it forward in new directions. It operates at many different layers. Sometimes it is highly localised, penetrating either short or deep time-scales. At others, it crosses national boundaries in pursuit of those global perspectives. Its debates are concerned with the tensions between visions of equilibrium and disruption, between notions of short-range transformations and degradations and longer-term cycles, between the construction of humans as dominating and destructive figures or what Crosby has called 'passive or distracted participants'. And issues of human instrumentality soon raise fundamental questions of power, of the capacity of empire, race and class to induce changes, whether intentionally or unwittingly, which benefit or damage the cultural and economic well-being of the different groups caught up in those power relationships.

These are the issues which these lectures address, primarily within the context of the British Empire. They identify some of the themes of recent studies, the different historiographical schools which have already emerged, and the possible direction of future research. They attempt to make a further contribution to the watershed year of 1995.

John M. MacKenzie
August 1996

NOTES

1. *Environment and History*, published by the White Horse Press in Cambridge from February 1995.
2. Simon Schama, *Landscape and Memory*, London 1995.
3. Richard Grove, *Green Imperialism: Colonial Expansion, Tropical Island Edens and the Origins of Environmentalism, 1600–1860*, Cambridge 1995.
4. David Arnold and Ramachandra Guha (eds.), *Nature, Culture, Imperialism: Essays on the Environmental History of South Asia*, Delhi 1995.
5. Jane Carruthers, *The Kruger National Park: a Social and Political History*, Pietermaritzburg 1995.
6. Geoff Park, *Nga Uruora: Ecology and History in a New Zealand Landscape*, Wellington 1995.
7. Tom Griffiths, *Hunters and Collectors: the Antiquarian Imagination in Australia*, Cambridge 1996.
8. Mahesh Rangarajan, 'Environmental Histories of South Asia', *Environment and History*, 2, 2 (1996), pp. 129–43.
9. Alfred Crosby, 'The Past and Present of Environmental History', *American Historical Review*, October 1995, pp. 1177–89.
10. Donald Worster, 'Doing Environmental History', in Donald Worster (ed.), *The Ends of the Earth: Perspectives on Modern Environmental History*, Cambridge 1988, pp. 289–307.
11. Grove, *Green Imperialism*, pp. 2–3 and 'North American innovation or imperial legacy?: contesting and re-assessing the roots and agendas of environmental history 1860–1996', a paper delivered at the Australian National University Colloquium on the Environment, February 1996.
12. Audrey I. Richards, *Land, Labour and Diet in Northern Rhodesia: an economic study of the Bemba Tribe*, London 1939.

The Historiography of Environmentalism: Apocalypse, neo-Whiggism and New Perspectives

I T is a particular honour to be asked to deliver the Callander Lectures in this your quincentennial year. Yet I cannot resist saying that I think it brave of you to invite a graduate of a university which celebrated *its* quincentennial forty-four years ago! But I hasten to add that in those years of post-war austerity, Glasgow could manage by way of celebration only a history by the redoubtable J. D. Mackie and a souvenir illustrated booklet.[1] There was nothing to compare with the historiographical explosion, under the expert detonation of Jennifer Carter, which has accompanied *your* quincentennial. Among all the riches, it has been my particular pleasure to read the illustrated history *Crown and Gown*, Paul Wood's *The Aberdeen Enlightenment*, and John Hargreaves's magnificent *Academe and Empire*.[2] The Callander Lectures are a distinguished series and the invitation to deliver them put me in mind of my favourite academic line. When I was an undergraduate at Glasgow in the early 1960s, there was a Professor of Moral Philosophy who, once a term, gripped his gown tightly and intoned 'My predecessor in my chair, Adam Smith ...' Looking at the list of those who have delivered these lectures, I cannot help feeling that with similar immodesty and almost equal incongruity, I could say 'My predecessors in my lectures ...'

Nevertheless, I believe that this year's lectures, in subject matter at least, constitute something of a fresh departure. Yet although environmental history is a comparatively new field of study, it conveniently brings together Thomas Callander's concerns with both war and imperialism. As long ago as 1896, Colonel Sir

Charles Callwell, the author of a celebrated handbook of colonial
warfare, *Small Wars*, remarked that such campaigns were essentially
'campaigns against nature'.[3] In a wider sense, imperial rule itself
was a campaign against nature, a major determinant of environmental change in all its aspects. In these lectures I shall be
examining a number of themes. In this first one, I shall consider
the manner in which modern anxieties about environmental threat
have coloured the past and not least the imperial past; I shall then
recount the development of the writing of environmental history
within the historiography of empire and I shall offer my estimation
of its strengths and weaknesses and the ways in which it may
extend and deepen its range in the future. In doing this I shall
be casting a sceptical eye upon some of the analytical extremes
to which we have been subjected in recent times. In the second
lecture, I shall question the notion of an imperial monolith and
consider the manner in which the rulers and experts of, and writers
about, empire reflected both supreme self-confidence and considerable doubt and anxiety in their approaches to their imperial
estate. I shall analyse some of the imperial policies which were
developed to respond to perceptions of environmental threat and
compare these with the green concerns of more modern times.
A running thread throughout will be the the role of empire as a
catalyst for changing attitudes towards fauna and flora, as well as
natural phenomena, together with the relationship of Scotland
and the Scots, not least graduates of this University, to these
developments. This theme will be particularly explored in the
final lecture when I shall look at the complexities of imperial
rule, ethnic contributions from above and below, the limitations
imposed upon policy, and approaches to the conceptualisation of
landscape.

THE ENDURING APOCALYPSE

Thomas Callander's book *The Athenian Empire and the British* is
an apocalyptic work. As so often happens with those who foresee

an apocalpyse, it emerged out of a dramatic conversion. When a young man, Callander accepted the tenets of Tory (and for that matter, Liberal) imperialism, excusing himself by referring to the power of the rhetoric of Rosebery, Ruskin, Rhodes, Tennyson and Kipling. In what could have been a blurb for my own work *Propaganda and Empire* of 1984, he remarked that 'The vast apparatus of publicity and indoctrination, schools and colleges, theatres and concert halls, the Press, the Churches, reviews and the book trade disseminated their [imperial] lessons'.[4]

Callander's apocalypse, in keeping with the historiographical obsessions of his age, was about the relationship between politics and warfare. The imperialism which had seemed to be such a righteous enterprise in the hands of its apologists and propagandists in the nineteenth century had become nothing but the generator of war and destruction in the twentieth. Although he did not make this explicit, a central idea lies behind his work: that the British had helped to create the major instrumental myth of the nineteenth and early twentieth centuries. This was that a great power, to develop its industrial nexus to the full, required an empire. It was that myth, or the propaganda derived from it, both of them only marginally connected with economic reality, which helped to drive the Germans into imperial expansionism between the 1880s and the First World War and the Americans into war with Spain in 1898. Its continuing potency impelled the Japanese into Manchuria in 1931, sent the Italians back into Ethiopia in 1935 and caused the German geographical and colonial societies, at times even the Europe-obsessed Hitler himself, to revive the German colonial claims in Africa and the Pacific in the late 1930s.[5]

For Callander, wars of aggression throughout history were 'au fond, imperialist'. As Thucydides and Tacitus, in their different Greek and Roman contexts, had pointed out, they were essentially about 'pleonexia', a Greek word which he translated as 'greed and grab', and constituted (in an almost ecological phrase) 'the moral corruption that has polluted our century'. If politicians did

not learn to adjust competing claims by diplomacy, then the future
of humans themselves was at stake.[6]

I have lingered on Callander's apocalypse because it connects
so neatly with the apocalyptic environmental vision which has
been such a part of our modern estimation of future risk. As wars
have become more localised than universal, the new 'pleonexia'
is about the greedy grabbing of rapidly diminishing natural resources, about the vast disparities between the affluent and the
under-developed, and about the emissions and pollutions through
which affluence is maintained. It is also about the exercise of post-
colonial power not just between the industrial and non-industrial
worlds, but also in the relationships of multi-national companies
and weak states, often mirroring the conflicting class interests of
rich and poor and of majorities and alternative life styles.[7] Less
frequently noticed, but very apparent to us in recent times, it is
also about conflict among pressure groups, experts, governments
and public opinions.

All apocalyptic visions have a tendency to colour interpretations
of history. Humans, it seems, not content with worrying about
the future, also worry about the past. The environmental movement has done this perhaps more than any other pressure group.
Its protagonists fret about their perception that people in history
failed to recognise the environmental disasters that were all around
them. And these people include not only those who allegedly
lived within rapidly degrading ecologies, but also those who
studied such societies in the late nineteenth and early twentieth
centuries. The latter, curiously blinded to the potential for environmental doom, sought out political, social or military
explanations for the decline of historic societies. Now, privileged
by our present apocalyptic insights, we can see that ecological
degradation explains almost everything.

For the environmentalists it is not just Apocalpyse Now, but
Apocalypse Then. And, in a reversal of the tendency in warfare,
if the then was localised, the now is globalised. Thus, the decline
and near-disappearance of Easter Island society, the abandonment

of the great cities and monumental structures of the Maya of Central America, the desertification of the Middle East and North Africa, the general degradation of the Mediterranean world, including Callander's Greece, the collapse of the state based upon Great Zimbabwe, the rapid deterioration of oceanic islands from the expansion of Europe in the fifteenth century onwards, and the strains imposed upon societies and cultures everywhere by the insatiable demands of agriculture throughout the world, all represent a foretaste of the doom that is to come. And they find it one of the anxious ironies of this revelation that the first visitors to Easter Island or the Maya monuments or to Great Zimbabwe, the first excavators of Ur and Harappa or Mohenjo-Daro failed to recognise something that their contemporaries were accelerating throughout the world: humans, particularly when gathered together in excessive numbers, place a strain upon their environment which it cannot sustain.

In this fearsome revelatory past, progressive and social evolutionary models have been turned on their heads. That vision of the stages of social and economic development, which itself partly came out of the study of comparative societies that was such a feature of the Scottish Enlightenment, has been replaced by a counter-progressive theory of startling proportions. Humans went wrong from the Neolithic revolution onwards. It was agriculture (sometimes together with over-enthusiastic pastoralism) that started the dry rot of the world; techniques like irrigation with its attendant salination turned it into wet rot; deforestation ate away at the supporting members and produced potentially fatal atmospheric changes; while finally industrialism and its associated imperialism undermined the very structure by insatiably exploiting resources above and below the surface of the earth, replacing them with all manner of chemical discharges.

This ultimate counter-progressive apocalypse, colouring the whole past with its fear of the future, fascinatingly seeks refuge in those very peoples who represented a primitive, doomed and unenviable barbarism to nineteenth- and twentieth-century exponents of empire. It is true that Captain Cook and Sir Joseph Banks, influenced by some of the noble savage perceptions of their age, at times (though not at others) found something appealing about the simplicity of the lives of Australian Aborigines.[8] More recently, that extraordinarily mystic late Romantic, Laurens van der Post, has celebrated the lives of the Bushmen of southern Africa.[9] But it was the distinguished American anthropologist Marshall Sahlins in his enthralling book, *Stone Age Economics*, who first described hunters and gatherers as 'the first affluent society'.[10] Though Sahlins did not moralise, those environmentalists who have been influenced by him appear at times to argue that all animal and crop domestications represented the true fall from grace. Our hunting and gathering past has become the only environmentally friendly Eden.

Visions of the Apocalypse are often exclusivist. Like millenarian religions, adherents for obvious reasons have to deny the validity of those that went before. In medieval and modern times, revelations have passed from religious to social, economic to technological, and political to military, culminating in the self-destructive terror of nuclear warfare. Now that we are once again close to the millennium, some of that sense of millenarian terror that was such a characteristic of medieval Europe in the year 1000 and at the end of other centuries is with us again. Yet what adds great power to the environmental apocalypse is the fact that it has the capacity to combine so many of those of the past. It has a spiritual content, even if a sort of modern pantheism or in religious terms a neo-primitivism; it also has significant social political, economic, technological and military dimensions. In its demographic fears it sometimes sounds like a case of extreme Malthusianism undreamt of by Malthus himself. It is a portmanteau apocalypse, sweeping up much of the content of those that have gone before it.

EMPIRE, THE APOCALYPSE AND THE
DEVELOPMENT OF A NEW HISTORIOGRAPHY

Such a vision of environmental evil requires a villain, and that role is unquestionably played by capitalism and its historic globalising vehicle, imperialism. I ought to interpolate here that although imperialism and empire are not necessarily co-terminous, for the purposes of this argument I propose to interchange them: throughout I mean a combination of what is often known as formal and informal empire. I should also explain that I shall be using the terms metropole and periphery to designate Britain and its imperial territories. If this language is somewhat patronising and a little outmoded, it remains a convenient geographical shorthand.

Those who have propounded the apocalypse argue that from its earliest days in the fifteenth century the expansion of Europe into the Atlantic and beyond served to globalise the acceleration of environmental change, and for them change means only one thing, persistent and rapid degradation. These effects, first felt with dramatic intensity in the Azores, Madeira and the Canaries, spread in turn to South and North America, the Caribbean, India, Australasia and the Pacific and finally Africa. Progressive stages of capitalism, agricultural, commercial and industrial, spread the concepts of ownership, beneficial exploitation for a royal or capitalist elite, and objectified and commoditised nature itself. The industrial revolution and modern market capitalism, with its insistent emphasis on growth rather than balance, dramatically accelerated these effects, particularly in the late nineteenth century.

There can be little doubt that the discipline of history has a tendency to respond to political controversy and successive waves of activism. We will better understand the emergence of imperial environmental history if we place it both in this polemical setting and also in the extraordinary broadening of the historical canvas in modern times. During the decades of a pronounced imperial historiography, from say the 1880s to the 1950s, intellectual challenges were mounted principally by economists, Marxists and, towards the end of the period, other disciplines like anthropology. It was the liberal journalist, J. A. Hobson – ironically a devoted admirer of the distinctly pro-imperial John Ruskin – and the Marxists who built on his analysis, culminating with that celebrated polemic of Lenin, who set the agenda for the first powerful response both to imperialism and the writing of its history.[11] Strikingly, it was a reaction which in the years just before, during and after the Second World War came as much from the West Indies as from the metropole, in the work of such figures as C. L. R. James and Eric Williams.[12] Major post-war economic studies, from Wallerstein to Fieldhouse, were to be noted for their sharply contrasting ideological commitments.[13]

Just as a fully fledged school of Marxist historians was beginning to emerge, history was again diverted into strongly political chan-nels by the development of what became known as the nationalist historiography in the 1960s. Its origins among Indian historians had been relatively anodyne, though there had been some striking re-interpretations of the 'Mutiny' of 1857.[14] But Africanists, at first mainly white practitioners, though soon joined by black colleagues, set about examining traditions of resistance to imperial rule.[15] Late nineteenth century movements, which the celebrated team of Robinson and Gallagher had referred to in 1963 as romantic, backward-looking and hopeless gestures of dying sys-tems, suddenly took on a new significance.[16] For some they were expressions of proto-nationalism, later becoming the inspiration of national parties, trade unions and the renewed resistance which led into decolonisation.

This nationalist historiography was heavily influenced by new forms of political, social and labour history in Europe. A pre-dominantly urban focus soon spread out into concerns with rural resistance and social change.[17] Indeed, the 'history from below' movement developed simultaneously in colonial as in metropolitan history. For the first time, perhaps, in these expressions of historio-graphical parallelism, it showed itself to be both methodologically and theoretically more sophisticated than its metropolitan counterpart.

Oral techniques, initially the preserve of anthropologists and so-called ethno-historians, were often first used by nationalist historians to question members of the elite, but soon became an essential part of the voicing of the unvoiced. Oral traditions were used to reconstruct pre-colonial history, if at times generating considerable debate about its biases and credibility.[18] Both nationalist history and initial concerns in the collection of pre-colonial traditions maintained a somewhat atavistic focus upon the development of state systems. So much so that at the height of this concentration upon individual states, one historian went so far as to suggest that the 'Humpty Dumpty' of imperial history had been shattered and that there was a major need to put him back together again.[19]

Like so many predictions, as we shall see in these lectures, this fear was swiftly proved wrong. Imperial history *was* welded, riveted and sticking plastered together again; and the reason I mention this range of remedial techniques is precisely because it happened on so many fronts. Historians of empire, influenced by many other disciplines as well as historiographical developments elsewhere, opened up a whole sequence of horizons that re-introduced the potential to integrate. These have included the cultural dimensions of empire, both in the realms of high and popular culture, the cultures of consensus and resistance in both metropole and colonial territories.[20] Post-colonial disillusion contributed to this revulsion from the state. Major schools in the writing of 'history from below', such as the 'Subaltern Studies' movement in India – heavily influenced by the theoretical writings of both Antonio Gramsci and Michel Foucault – were representative of this reaction, as was the development of gender studies.[21] We have also become more interested in the intellectual and scientific histories of empire, recognising the manner in which both science and ideas are deeply implicated in the power relations of imperial rule. It is indeed one of the most encouraging aspects of the modern historiography that the histories of science and medicine which, until comparatively recently, were somewhat esoteric areas of study, have joined the mainstream of intellectual history.[22] Empire and modern science forged a significant alliance from the mid-eighteenth to the mid-twentieth centuries.[23] Not only were imperial territories the greatest laboratory ever handed to scientists, but they also served to encourage the fanning out of older disciplines and the spawning of new ones, from geology to geography, botany to entomology, zoology to forestry, hydrography to tropical medicine, anthropology to philology, agronomy to museology, a far from exhaustive list. This has been accompanied by a renewed interest in technology, analysed partly as a marker of European superiority, partly and more controversially as the major instrument of imperial expansion.[24] Through these developments, it is now apparent that the imperial experience was much more than a one-way process: the radiation of influences outwards was profoundly modified, in both cultural and scientific forms, by the periphery. This could only happen because the cultural, political, intellectual and institutional life of the metropolis itself was influenced by the possession of empire.

Perhaps it is an indication of the narrowness of English education and the rather blinkered approach of historians that, until quite recently, scholars missed so much of the disciplinary and ideological complexities that have now been recognised as essential to a full understanding of imperialism. It is a melancholy fact that the leading standard single-volume texts on the history of the British empire remain in the old mould of political, economic, military and administrative history.[25] Now there is another new development whereby disaggregation can help re-integration. This is the recognition that British rulers, experts and migrants in the empire were not themselves a homogeneous group. They came from very different social, cultural, educational and intellectual backgrounds within the United Kingdom. This has long been recognised in migration studies, not least by scholars at this university, but the notion of a specifically Scottish contribution

to Empire, though noted by many imperial writers in the nineteenth and twentieth centuries, has only recently come to be
analysed in new ways.[26] I shall be returning to this theme in the
third lecture.

THE DEVELOPMENT OF THE
ENVIRONMENTAL HISTORY OF EMPIRE

It was, then, in the context of both the politicisation of the
environment and this dramatic expansion of historical interests
that the environmental history of the empire became one of the
most rapid of the new growths. In the space of little more than
two decades it has already formed up into specific schools and
specialisms. The first of these, perhaps inevitably, took imperial
claims of the beneficent effects of western technology, science
and medicine, and turned them upside down.

This is neatly illustrated by a pioneering work on the great
canal systems of British India which was published by Elizabeth
Whitcombe in 1972.[27] She argued that those canals, which were
so symbolic of British power and its inheritance from the
Mughals, produced a very different effect from that intended. The
British sought to increase the land revenue, the fiscal basis of
their power, by greater environmental control. To overcome the
intermittent precipitation and water shortages of north-western
India they rebuilt and massively extended the canal systems of the
Jumna, Ganges and Indus river systems. They also turned their
attention to such rivers as the Cauvery and Godavery in the
Madras presidency. By doing so they would create the opportunity for more extensive agricultural settlements in those
regions and improve the general lot of the peasantry. The result,
wrote Whitcombe, using British data including the observations
of irrigation officers, was very different. Because both the system and its execution were misconceived, they produced not
economic regeneration, but extensive and damaging waterlogging
as well as high levels of salination akin to those produced in

ancient Middle Eastern irrigation systems which had similarly
gone wrong.

In the same year, 1972, Alfred Crosby published his *The Columbian Exchange*, examining the export of plants, animals and
diseases to the Americas from Europe.[28] He expanded this con-
siderably in his *Ecological Imperialism* of 1986, where he argued
that organisms of all sorts were marshalled, wittingly and unwittingly, in the progressive European conquest of the globe.[29]
Mammals, birds, freshwater fish, insects, pathogens, trees, plants,
weeds were all carried by Europeans throughout the world, for
economic, aesthetic, sporting or simply nostalgic reasons. For
Crosby, this resulted in the creation of Neo-Europes, exotic
environments comprehensively overlaid with the extensive biota
of the new conquerors. He paid little or no attention to Africa
and argued that only the well-established historic peasant cultures
of Asia resisted this effect, a contention that some modern scholars
deny. What is more, Crosby argued, highly dubiously, that the
surprising thing was that so little came back. In his determination
to see biological imperialism as a one-way process, illustrated by
the imperialist urges of the dandelion, he seemed to know little
of the expansion of the eucalyptus or the Australian wattle, the
depredations of the rhododendron, Japanese knotweed, or Himalayan balsam, the territorial hunger of the grey squirrel, the mink
or the New Zealand flat worm.

Writing in the late 1970s, another American scholar, Lucile
Brockway, had already provided a conspiratorial twist to this
biological expansion by concerning herself with the role of continental and inter-continental plant transfers, such as tea and opium,
rubber, cinchona and sisal in the development of plantation economies and world capitalism.[30] She saw these exchanges as being
part of a global plot, masterminded by scientific controllers at
Kew Gardens, involving the often secret removal of economic
plants from regions which were either relatively inaccessible or
beyond European political control to colonial territories where
they could be subjected to plantation techniques.

Those very plantations not only created new forms of indentured labour and slavery, but also had a devastating effect on forests and soil qualities, and this became another major concern of environmental historians of the apocalyptic school.[31] Plantation crops are land extensive and soil intensive. They generally have high energy demands, for example in sugar boiling and tobacco curing. They create monocultures which store up social and political, economic and environmental problems over time. Moreover, plantations continued to be created almost throughout the entire life history of imperial rule. From the Atlantic islands they spread to the Caribbean, North and South America, Indian Ocean islands, India, Australia, South and East Africa. The forests of Mauritius, Sri Lanka, the Nilgiri hills of south India, the Himalayan foothills, Queensland, Natal, Zimbabwe and Malawi fell to the ever insatiable demands of sugar, coffee, tea, cinchona, and tobacco. A large proportion of the Malayan peninsula saw its natural landscape overwhelmed by rubber trees in the decade or two before the First World War. It was an imperial process still in full swing in the inter-war years of this century and beyond.

Studies of East and Central Africa powerfully developed this sense of imperial catastrophe. As early as 1977 the Swedish scholar Helge Kjekshus published his *Ecology Control and Economic Development in East African History* with its strongly contrasting images of a period of plenty in pre-colonial times shattered by a series of environmental and medical disasters attendant upon the arrival of Europeans in the 1890s.[32] Some of these, like rinderpest (which afflicted cattle and game including buffalo and the larger antelopes), smallpox and jigger fleas were directly introduced, albeit inadvertently, by European agency. Others like the prevalence of drought and the spreading of locust swarms happened to coincide with the appearance of Europeans, leading contemporary Africans to draw appropriate spiritual conclusions. Others again like the spread of trypanosomiasis and East Coast fever among cattle and sleeping sickness among humans were spread through misconceived colonial policies.[33] In rather more sophisticated studies spanning parts of Zambia, Malawi and Mozambique, Leroy Vail has argued that a 'major ecological catastrophe' resulted from the combined impact of expanding capitalism and colonial administration in the region.[34] If some evidence of pre-colonial problems can be identified, then imperial rule seized a system that was already under stress and pushed it over the edge.

Kjekshus has rightly been criticised for creating a vision of Merrie Africa, and indeed parallel images of Merrie Australia and Merrie India can be identified in the literature. William Lines's *Taming the Great South Land*, published in 1991, is a record of rapine and plunder, of the piling of environmental disaster upon natural catastrophe since the arrival of Europeans in Australasia.[35] It is notably more lurid in its approach that Geoffrey Bolton's pioneering *Spoils and Spoilers*, published ten years earlier, which pulls no punches, but achieves a certain degree of balance.[36] Mahev Gadgil and Ramachandra Guha's standard environmental history of India, *This Fissured Land* of 1991, creates a theory of modes of resource use to illustrate the greater harmony between humans and nature in the pre-imperial period. They argue that conservation ideas were more highly developed both among the rulers of India and among hunters, pastoralists and cultivators dependent for their survival upon natural resources, than they were among western intruders.[37]

Gadgil and Guha, in common with many environmental historians in Asia, have laid a great deal of stress upon forests. Mirroring contemporary concerns about the Amazon and elsewhere, they have identified the forest as being the prime locus of imperial destruction, for cultivation, naval building, and the very considerable demands of domestic and industrial fuel. In British India, everywhere from the celebrated hill station of Simla to the great city of Madras made stunning fuel demands upon their surrounding and more distant woodlands.[38] What is more, the development of the new steam technology, far from bringing relief, ravaged forests yet further: engines sometimes burnt wood despite its massive inefficiencies, but much more significantly the

laying of railway lines created a demand for literally millions of
sleepers, which in tropical climates often needed to be replaced
every five to ten years.[39] Moreover, it was the command of forests
that most clearly represented British power over the landscape
and their capacity to control and transform the lives of those
peoples who lived within them.

Yet it is also in relation to forests that a counter movement to
the notion of imperial disaster has emerged. I call this the 'development of sensibilities' school. It extends the work of a number of
scholars who have identified shifts in both social sensitivities and
reactions to nature across the eighteenth-nineteenth century
divide. Norbert Elias first identified this in his *The Civilising Process:
the History of Manners*, published in 1939.[40] My former colleague,
Harold Perkin, produced a classic statement of it in his *The Origins
of Modern English Society*:

> Between 1780 and 1850 the English ceased to be one of the most
> aggressive, brutal, rowdy, outspoken, riotous, cruel and bloodthirsty
> nations in the world and became one of the most inhibited, polite,
> orderly, tenderminded, prudish and hypocritical.[41]

Keith Thomas carried this notion into the English – and his work
was highly Anglo-centric – relationship with nature. He identified
a 'revolution in perceptions' associated with Romanticism and the
development of Enlightenment and post-Enlightenment science.
The result was 'to create new sensibilities that have gained in
intensity ever since'.[42] David Allen in charting the rise of natural
history as a popular pursuit, together with the societies founded
by its practitioners, has also seen this as symptomatic of new
responses to nature. He simply moves Thomas's reassuring Romantic climacteric further into the nineteenth century.[43] Even
Harriet Ritvo, in her book *The Animal Estate*, though rightly
approaching the human relationship with animals both in terms
of power and of class, saw growing sensitivities emerging by the
end of the century.[44]

In many respects, Richard Grove's new book, with its defiant title, *Green Imperialism*, fits into this tradition.[45] Grove asserts that locating the origins of environmentalism in the United States, in the writings of George Perkins Marsh, John Muir, Henry David Thoreau and others is yet another example of Yankee intellectual imperialism.[46] For Grove, environmental ideas not only have a greater antiquity, they also emerge from the colonial periphery. Thus metropolitan science learns much from the imperial experience, initially in oceanic islands and later in India. In charting the development of desiccation theory and anxieties about deforestation and species extinction from the seventeenth to the mid-nineteenth centuries, he demonstrates the international character of research in colonial ecologies. By a neat analytical sleight of hand he links such ideas to radical politics in the late eighteenth century. Moreover, he sees their transference into the British consciousness as occurring through the agency of the Indian Medical Service, whose botanist doctors, so many of them trained here in Aberdeen, were the main propagators of these ideas within the British Empire.

Grove's work, though it seldom makes concessions to accessibility, has considerable strengths. He has globalised so successfully that he has done primary work on the Caribbean, oceanic islands in both the Atlantic and Indian Oceans, the Cape and India. His Humpty Dumpty shows barely a crack. Indeed, one reviewer remarked that Grove's scholarly travels made Marco Polo look like a layabout. He has carried the story back to the seventeenth century and he has also identified the different intellectual strands, including a very considerable Scottish one, that come together into the fabric of enlightened environmental thought. But the minute tracing of the development and explication of such ideas too often leaves out of account the extent to which they were applied. Application occurs within political, social and cultural contexts that impose constraints and barriers that also need to be fully appreciated. *Green Imperialism* ends in 1860, at just the time when imperial rule is moving into a fresh phase. Grove has taken account of this in other publications, but his analysis follows the neo-Whiggish inclinations of Thomas, rather like Christopher Smout's search for 'the Roots of Green Consciousness' in the Scottish Highlands.[47]

You will have gathered by now that I have considerable reservations about both the apocalyptic and the neo-Whiggish approaches, reservations that I shall explore more fully in my second lecture. Does the historiography offer any alternative routes? Indeed it does. In the past few years, there has been a positive plethora of publications in the environmental histories of the British and other empires. Much of this work has demonstrated that perspectives and time-scales are opening up. The lengthening of the post-colonial era has reduced the tendency to see the imperial experience as both uniquely transformatory and peculiarly destructive. The publication a few years ago of a book with the title *The Colonial Moment in Africa* indicates the extent to which some see the imperial experience in that Continent at any rate as representing only a tiny part of its history.[48] Just as an aside, when I collected oral evidence in what is now Zimbabwe in the early 1970s, I frequently met elderly informants who had reached maturity before imperial rule had arrived. We do well to remember that many people in Africa lived to see both the beginning and the end of the colonial era.

A great deal of this new work has been concerned with fragile ecologies, with forest and marginal zones, with regions of transhumant pastoralism, with faunal extinctions and survivals, with issues involving the relationships between peoples and power, demographic and climatic change and the incidence of famine.[49] Gender approaches, discussing the respective roles of men and women in the environment, have also been developed.[50] Much of this research has tended to see the changes wrought by imperial power as but one phase in much longer cycles of environmental ups and downs not unlike those of the 'dismal science' of economics. Indeed, indigenous knowledge in many regions of Asia, Africa and Australasia reveals that many peoples have their own awareness of some form of the biblical cycle of feast and famine.

Although climatic history has yet to catch up with the varied approaches to past climates in several of the natural sciences, archaeologists and historians do now deal in the currency of pluvials and inter-pluvials, little Ice Ages, volcanic and El Nino-induced transformations.[51]

A number of interim conclusions have already emerged from some of this research. Pre-colonial peoples had more power to transform their environments, mainly through fire, than imperial rulers allowed. This is true of Australia, India and Africa. Very probably there were pre-colonial species extinctions through over-hunting and, at times, profligate killing. One or two have been identified in Australia.[52] The arrival of new migrant peoples, like the Bantu-speakers in Africa, or dominant elites in India, had the capacity to transform the environment as much as, or even more than, colonial rulers, not least because they had a longer time to achieve it. Hunters and gatherers were, perhaps, well aware of this: there is a Bushman cave painting not far from Harare which, very movingly, shows an immigrant Bantu-speaker cutting down a tree with an axe, something inconceivable to the hunter, in both technical and environmental terms. The repeated incidence of dearth may well have produced demographic swings and it is at least possible in the African case that Europeans arrived during an environmental downturn, which both indigenous contempor-aries and modern protagonists of the apocalyptic view wrongly attributed to their agency. Thus we have to understand the mutual effects and complex oscillations of both the natural cycle and human-induced change. We now know more of the historical depth of famine in, for example, both Ethiopia and India, knowl-edge which in both cases goes back to at least the sixteenth century.[53]

We know that deforestation is far from being just a modern phenomenon; nor is the tight control of forests, their resources and who may live there. Successor states to the Mughals in India may have developed forest policies which became a model for the British at a later date.[54] There has been a good deal of speculation about the extent to which environmental problems had effects not only on a medieval state like Zimbabwe, but also on eighteenth and nineteenth century states in Zululand, Angola and Malawi. At the same time, scholars have just begun to question whether the ancient Indus civilisations did in fact collapse as a result of a self-induced environmental crisis.[55]

Others have pointed to the complex diversity of the imperial impact. It has been suggested that capitalism interacted with, rather than dominated, environments, producing a mix of deleterious and favourable outcomes.[56] At times, indigenous peoples succeeded in frustrating attempts at environmental protection – examples have been found in both West and East Africa.[57] What's more, the imperial monolith has increasingly fragmented. Sometimes, rulers and experts tried desperately to settle nomadic pastoralists, not always with success; elsewhere pastoralists were culturally valued more highly than the supposedly softer, stationary peasantry. Some colonial authorities in Africa sought to destroy game to try to beat back the incidence of the tsetse fly which used game as a host; others created vast national parks to encourage the regeneration of game stocks.[58] The presence or otherwise of settlers was crucial to these disparities in policy. Towards the end of imperial rule there were at least the beginnings of a better understanding of the inter-relationship between forest peoples and their environment and between pastoralists, their herds and game. The nationalist historiography has often influenced environmental historians into concentrating on instances of resistance when submission and collaboration may have been just as prominent a part of indigenous response. In many instances, post-colonial states have been more a prey to sectional interests than imperial rulers, more concerned to settle nomads, and also more subject to powerful international conservation lobbies that do not always take indigenous needs into account.[59]

But although these are all necessary correctives, we should not of course go too far. We should always remember that throughout history, one person's conservation has often been another person's dispossession. We should also be reminded of the fact that all conservation ideas and policies have to be set within a wider cultural framework as well as the complex interaction of power relationships, involving class as well as race, economic, intellectual and institutional interest groups, and the quest of administrators for that perfect combination of justificatory ideals and the quiet life. Thus we should remember that empires of nature are deeply embedded in the nature of empires.

We should also remember, as we saw earlier in the lecture, that much scholarly activity tends to be skewed by prominent contemporary concerns. It is, for example, very noticeable that all this wealth of environmental history has concentrated heavily on forests and their management, on interior land use, soil degradation and, in some instances, the relationship between people and animals. Much less work has been done on coastal and riverine ecologies, on fisheries, such marine activities in Asia and the Pacific as pearling (a particular fascination of mine), city and town environments, surely a major aspect of environmental history and concern, and many of the wider aspects of faunal change. The tropics have also come in for more attention than the temperate and Arctic zones, for example in northern Canada. Indeed, it is a curious fact that Canadian historians have not yet attempted an integrated environmental history.

I have identified, then, three strands in the writing of imperial environmental history. The first of these, which I have called the apocalyptic, represents the first historical response to the beginnings of the green controversies of the 1960s and 1970s. But while the apocalyptic polemic has remained politically useful to the Green Movement, historians have, generally, moved on. My second strand was the one I dubbed neo-Whiggish, a longer-standing tradition which still has its modern, even recent practitioners. It too is influenced by green politics, to the extent that it sees modern sensibilities as an enlightened form of ecological awareness, the roots of which can be found in the cultural histories of both manners and ideas in the past. Both the apocalyptic and neo-Whiggish approaches tend to share a Euro-centric focus. For the first, European imperialism is both all-powerful and all-destructive, an environmental Götterdämmerung of Wagnerian proportions. For the second, the West is privileged by its discovery of ecological sensitivities. The first sometimes highlights, the second downplays or ignores research on both the sensitivities of Asian philosophies and religions and the extent of indigenous environmental knowledge throughout the world.[60]

In my third strand, historians seek to adopt a longer perspective, recognising that the era of European imperialism represents but a brief period in the history of the human interaction with tropical and sub-tropical ecologies, and noting that many of the problems identified through the wealth of imperial data can be seen to represent the recurrence of difficulties that archaeological, oral and natural science techniques reveal to have been endemic in the pre-colonial past. Of course, this does not solve our problem. Superficially, we seem to have radical challenge, neo-Whiggish response, and a new balance. But this begs all sorts of questions. It is still possible that imperial transformations, though necessarily to be set into a longer time-frame, still represent more severe disruptions in both qualitative and quantitative terms. They may also indicate a speeding-up, even a dangerous acceleration, of the human-induced changes which clearly interact with the climatic and other natural cycles that both indigenous knowledge and modern science are all too aware of in their differing ways.

In my next two lectures, I shall be looking more closely at the environmental effects of imperial rule and the ways in which both the sense of control over nature and also perceptions of crisis influenced the scale and nature of policy. I shall also develop the notion, mentioned earlier, of a distinctive contribution by Scots to the development of environmental ideas, albeit within the cultural contexts of their times. Moreover, it may well be that the conceptualisation of the Scottish environment influenced colonial concepts, while the imperial experience transmitted ideas back to Scotland.

Meanwhile, to shift the focus to contemporary times, it is surely the case that if any part of Michael Hechter's 'internal colonialism' survives in relation to Scotland it is in the area of land ownership and environmental change.[61] Even in the fastnesses of 'imperial' England, I am able to follow the intriguing environmental obsessions of the newspaper, *Scotland on Sunday*. I shall attempt an explanation of these connections in my third lecture.

NOTES TO LECTURE ONE

1. J. D Mackie, *The University of Glasgow 1451–1951*, Glasgow, 1954 was published three years after the quincentennial. The illustrated booklet, *Glasgow University Through Five Centuries*, was published by the University in 1951. More recently, A. L. Brown and Michael Moss, *The University of Glasgow: 1451–1996*, Edinburgh, 1996 has appeared, but it lacks references or sources and is of limited value to scholars.

2. Jennifer J. Carter and Colin A. McLaren, *Crown and Gown 1495–1995*, Aberdeen, 1994; Paul B. Wood, *The Aberdeen Enlightenment: the Arts Curriculum in the Eighteenth Century*, Aberdeen. 1993; John D. Hargreaves, *Academe and Empire: Some overseas Connections of Aberdeen University 1860–1970*, Aberdeen, 1994. The latter complements the same author's *Aberdeenshire to Africa: Northeast Scots and British Overseas Expansion*, Aberdeen 1981.

3. C. E. Callwell, *Small Wars: their Principles and Practice*, London 1906, p. 98.

4. Thomas Callander, *The Athenian Empire and the British*, London 1961, p. 26.

5. See, for example, L. S. Amery, *The German Colonial Claim*, London, 1939.

6. Callander, *Athenian Empire*, pp. 113, 118, 169, 171.

7. See, for example, Clive Ponting, *A Green History of the World*, Harmondsworth 1991. For more respectable surveys, see I. G. Simmons, *Environmental History: a Concise Introduction*, Oxford 1993 and, from a geographical perspective, A. M. Mannion, *Global Environmental Change: a Natural and Cultural Environmental History*, London 1991.

8. Bernard Smith, *European Vision and the South Pacific*, London 1985, p. 169.

9. Laurens van der Post, *The Lost World of the Kalahari*, London 1958 and *The Heart of the Hunter*, London 1961.

10. Marshall Sahlins, *Stone Age Economics*, Chicago 1972.

11. J. A. Hobson, *Imperialism – a Study*, London 1902; V. I. Lenin, *Imperialism, the Highest Stage of Capitalism*, first published 1916 or 1917; and the critique of this literature in D. K. Fieldhouse, *The Theory of Capitalist Imperialism*, London 1967.

12. Eric Williams, *Capitalism and Slavery*, London 1944; C. L. R. James, *The Case for West Indian Self-Government*, London 1933; *The Black Jacobins: Toussaint Louverture and the San Domingo Revolution*, London 1938 and *A History of Negro Revolt*, London 1938.

13. Immanuel Wallerstein, *The Modern World System*, especially vols II and III, *Mercantilism and the Consolidation of the European World Economy, 1600–1750*, New York 1980 and *The Second Era of Great Expansion of the Capitalist World Economy, 1730–1840s*, London 1989; also *The Capitalist World Economy: Essays*, Cambridge 1979; D. K. Fieldhouse, *Economics and Empire 1839–1914*, London 1973 and *The Colonial Empires: a Comparative Survey from the Eighteenth Century*, London 1966.

14. S. N. Sen, *Eighteen Fifty Seven*, New Delhi 1957; V. D. Savarkar, *The Indian War of Independence*, Delhi 1857; Eric Stokes, *The Peasant Armed: the Indian Revolt of 1857*, ed. by C. A. Bayly, Oxford 1986.

15. T. O. Ranger, *Revolt in Southern Rhodesia 1896–97*, Oxford 1967; Robert I. Rotberg and Ali A. Mazrui (eds.), *Protest and Power in Black Africa*, Oxford 1970.

16. R. Robinson and J. Gallagher, 'The Partition of Africa', in F. H. Hinsley (ed.), *The New Cambridge Modern History*, vol. XI, Cambridge 1962, pp. 593–640, particularly p. 640.

17. Eric Stokes, 'Rural Revolt in the Great Rebellion of 1857 in India', in *Historical Journal*, xii (1969) and *The Peasant and the Raj: studies in agrarian society and peasant rebellion in colonial India*, Cambridge 1978. This approach has been much developed by the Subaltern Studies school of Indian historians (see footnote 21 below). See also William Beinart and Colin Bundy, *Hidden Struggles in Rural South Africa*, London 1987.

18. See for example David P. Henige, *Chronology of Oral Tradition: Quest for a Chimera*, Oxford 1974; *Oral Historiography*, London 1974.

19. D. K. Fieldhouse, '"Can Humpty-Dumpty be put together again?" Imperial History in the 1980s', *Journal of Imperial and Commonwealth History*, XI, 2 (1984), pp. 9–23.

20. John M. MacKenzie, *Propaganda and Empire*, Manchester 1984 and

(as editor), *Imperialism and Popular Culture*, Manchester 1986, as well as other works in the Manchester University Press 'Studies in Imperialism' series.

21. Ranajit Guha, *Elementary Aspects of Peasant Insurgency in Colonial India*, New Delhi 1983; Ranajit Guha and Gayatri Chakravorty Spivak (eds.), *Selected Subaltern Studies*, New York 1989, which included essays from the subaltern studies volumes issued in New Delhi in 1982, '83, '84, '85 and '87.

22. There is now a considerable literature on science and empire. Early work includes Carlo M. Cipolla, *European Culture and Overseas Expansion*, Harmondsworth 1970 and Kurt Mendelssohn, *Science and Western Domination*, London 1976. More recently, see Roy MacLeod and Philip F. Rehbock (eds.), *Nature in its Greatest Extent: Western Science in the Pacific*, Honolulu 1988; Roy MacLeod (ed.), *The Commonwealth of Science: ANZAAS and the Scientific Enterprise in Australia, 1888–1988*, Melbourne 1988; Deepak Kumar (ed.), *Science and Empire, Essays in Indian Context (1700–1947)*, Delhi 1991; Satpal Sangwan, *Science, Technology and Colonisation, an Indian Experience 1757–1857*, Delhi 1991; Robert A. Stafford, *Scientist of Empire: Sir Roderick Murchison, scientific exporation and Victorian Imperialism*, Cambridge 1989; John M. MacKenzie (ed.), *Imperialism and the Natural World*, Manchester 1992; and Michael A. Osborne, *Nature, the Exotic and the Science of French Colonialism*, Bloomington, Indiana, 1994. The importance of cattle and other animal diseases in human history has long been recognised: for a recent study with important environmental and imperial connections, see Paul F. Cranefield, *Science and Empire: East Coast fever in Rhodesia and the Transvaal*, Cambridge 1991. An excellent discussion of theoretical shifts can be found in Paulo Palladino and Michael Worboys, 'Science and Imperialism', *Isis*, 84 (1993), pp. 91–102.

23. See, for example, George Stocking, *Victorian Anthropology*, New York 1987; Anne Godlewska and Neil Smith (eds.), *Geography and Empire*, Oxford 1994, and Morag Bell, Robin Butlin and Mike Heffernan (eds.), *Geography and Imperialism, 1820–1940*, Manchester 1995.

24. Daniel R. Headrick, *The Tools of Empire: Technology and European Imperialism in the Nineteenth Century*, Oxford 1981 and *The Tentacles of Progress: Technology Transfer in the Age of Imperialism, 1850–1940*, Oxford 1988.

25. T. O. Lloyd, *The British Empire 1558–1983*, Oxford 1984. Even the more recent editions of Bernard Porter, *The Lion's Share, a Short*

History of British Imperialism, London 1975 have maintained this focus. Denis Judd, *Empire, the British Imperial Experience from 1765 to the Present*, London 1996 makes some attempt to break the mould, at least in cultural terms. Scientific and environmental history are, however, still ignored. The environment is approached mainly through the media of art and economics in P. J. Marshall (ed.), *Cambridge Illustrated History of the British Empire*, Cambridge 1996. The new multi-volume *Oxford History of the British Empire*, to be published in 1998 under the general editorship of W. Roger Louis, should represent the first major attempt to escape the old pattern, though it has already been criticised by Lord Beloff for its temerity in attempting such innovation and its excursions into these fields may still seem somewhat tentative.

26. John M. MacKenzie, 'On Scotland and the Empire', *The International History Review*, XV, 4 (1993), pp. 714–39 and R. A. Cage (ed.), *The Scots Abroad*, London 1985. Among studies of emigration, Marjory Harper, *Emigration from North-East Scotland*, 2 vols, Aberdeen 1988, is outstanding.

27. Elizabeth Whitcombe, *Agrarian Conditions in Northern India*, 2 vols, Berkeley, California, 1972.

28. Alfred W. Crosby, *The Columbian Exchange: Biological and Cultural Consequences of 1492*, Westport, Connecticut, 1972.

29. Alfred W. Crosby, *Ecological Imperialism: the Biological Expansion of Europe, 900–1900*, Cambridge 1986.

30. Lucile H. Brockway, *Science and Colonial Expansion: the Role of the British Royal Botanical Gardens*, New York 1979.

31. Crosby, *Ecological Imperialism*, chapter 4 deals with the environmental effects of the plantation system on Atlantic islands and, by extension, elsewhere in the world.

32. Helge Kjekshus, *Ecology Control and Economic Development in East African History*, London 1977.

33. John Ford, *The Role of Trypanosomiases in African Ecology: a Study of the Tsetse Fly Problem*, Oxford 1971; John M. MacKenzie, 'Experts and Amateurs: tsetse, nagana and sleeping sickness in East and Central Africa', in MacKenzie (ed.), *Imperialism and the Natural World*, pp. 187–212.

34. Leroy Vail, 'Ecology and History: the example of Eastern Zambia', *Journal of Southern African Studies*, 3 (1977), pp. 129–55; 'The political economy of East-Central Africa', in D. Birmingham and P. M. Martin (eds.), *History of Central Africa*, London 1983, vol. 2, pp. 200–50.

35. William Lines, *Taming the Great South Land: A History of the Conquest of Nature in Australia*, London 1991.

36. Geoffrey Bolton, *Spoils and Spoilers: Australians Make their Environment, 1788–1980*, Sydney 1981.

37. Madhav Gadgil and Ramachandra Guha, *This Fissured Land: An Ecological History of India*, Oxford 1992. But see also Michael Mann, 'Ecological Change in North India: Deforestation and Agrarian Distress in the Ganga-Jamna Doab 1800–1850', in *Environment and History*, 1, 2 (1995), pp. 201–20 for the Mughal roots of environmental degradation.

38. Gadgil and Guha, *Fissured Land*, passim; Richard P. Tucker, 'The depletion of India's forests under British imperialism: planters, foresters, and peasants in Assam and Kerala', in Worster (ed.), *Ends of the Earth*, pp. 118–40. For the fuel demands of Simla and Madras, see E. P. Stebbing, *Forests of India*, 2 vols, London 1922, pp. 283–4 and 311.

39. Gadgil and Guha, *Fissured Land*, pp. 121–2.

40. Norbert Elias, *The Civilising Process, the History of Manners*, translated by Edmund Jephcott, Oxford 1978 (first published Basle 1939).

41. Harold J. Perkin, *The Origins of Modern English Society*, London 1969, p. 280.

42. Keith Thomas, *Man and the Natural World: Changing Attitudes in England, 1500–1800*, London 1983, pp. 15, 243.

43. D. E. Allen, *The Naturalist in Britain, a Social History*, London 1976.

44. Harriet Ritvo, *The Animal Estate: the English and other Creatures in the Victorian Age*, Harmondsworth 1990 (first published in 1987).

45. Richard Grove, *Green Imperialism*.

46. The articles cited by Crosby and Worster in footnotes 9 and 10 of the introduction maintain this concentration on American scholarship. Worster makes a nod in the direction of the French *Annales* School, but neither acknowledges work on the British Empire.

47. T. C. Smout, 'The Highlands and the Roots of Green Consciousness, 1750–1990', the Raleigh Lecture on History, *Proceedings of the British Academy*, 76 (1991), pp. 237–63. 'Roots' is a common word in environmental titles: David Pepper, *The Roots of Modern Environmentalism*, London 1984.

48. Andrew Roberts, *The Colonial Moment in Africa*, Cambridge 1990.

49. Examples of this work can be found in David Anderson and Richard Grove (eds.), *Conservation in Africa: people, policies and practice*, Cambridge 1987 and Douglas Johnson and David Anderson (eds.), *The*

Ecology of Survival: Case Studies from Northeast African History, London 1988.

50. See, for example, Henrietta L Moore and Megan Vaughan, *Cutting Down Trees: Gender, Nutrition and Agricultural Change in the Northern Province of Zambia, 1890–1990*, London 1994 and Francine Hughes, 'Conflicting uses for forest resources in the Lower Tana River basin of Kenya', in Anderson and Grove (eds.), *Conservation*, pp. 211–28, an article which also stresses the importance of women researchers interviewing women on fuel wood needs.

51. See, for example, Raymond S. Bradley and Philip D. Jones (eds.), *Climate since 1500*, London 1992.

52. Bolton, *Spoils and Spoilers*, pp. 6–7. For indigenous overhunting, see also Gadgil and Guha, *This Fissured Land*, p. 73 and William Beinart and Peter Coates, *Environment and History: the taming of nature in the USA and South Africa*, London 1995, pp. 4, 20.

53. R. Pankhurst, *The History of Famine and Epidemics in Ethiopia Prior to the Twentieth Century*, Addis Ababa 1985 and C. A. Wood, 'A preliminary chronology of Ethiopian droughts', in D. Dalby, R. J. Harrison Church, F. Bezzaz (eds.), *Drought in Africa 2*, African Environmental Special Report 6, International African Institute, London 1977. For a review of the literature of famine, see David Arnold, *Famine: Social Crisis and Historical Change*, Oxford 1988.

54. Chetan Singh, 'Forests, Pastoralists and Agrarian Society in Mughal India' and Atluri Murali, 'Whose Trees? Forest Practices and Local Communities in Andhra, 1600–1922', both in Arnold and Guha (eds.), *Nature, Culture, Imperialism*, pp. 21–48 and 86–122. Continuities have also been noted between British forest policy and that of independent India. Gadgil and Guha, *This Fissured Land* and Ramachandra Guha, *The Unquiet Woods: Ecological Change and Peasant Resistance in the Himalaya*, Delhi 1989.

55. Gadgil and Guha, *This Fissured Land*, p. 78.

56. John McCracken, 'Colonialism, capitalism and ecological crisis in Malawi: a reassessment', in Anderson and Grove (eds.), *Conservation in Africa*, pp. 63–77; 'Planters, Peasants and the Colonial State: the Impact of the Native Tobacco Board in the Central Province of Malawi', in the *Journal of Southern African Studies*, 9, 2 (1983), pp. 172–92.

57. Andrew Millington, 'Environmental degradation, soil conservation and agricultural policies in Sierra Leone, 1895–1984' and David Anderson, 'Managing the Forest, the Conservation history of

Lembus, Kenya, 1904–1963', in Anderson and Grove (eds.), *Conservation in Africa*, pp. 229–48 and 249–68.

58. John M. MacKenzie, *The Empire of Nature: Hunting, Conservation and British Imperialism*, Manchester 1988, chapters 9 and 10. See also William Beinart, 'Empire, Hunting and Ecological Change in Southern and Central Africa', in *Past and Present*, no. 128 (1990), pp. 162–86. An entire issue of the *Journal of Southern Africa Studies* (15, 2, 1989) was devoted to this and similar issues.

59. Olusegun Areola, 'The political reality of conservation in Nigeria', in Anderson and Grove (eds.), *Conservation in Africa*, pp. 277–92; Madhav Gadgil and Ramachandra Guha, *Ecology and Equity: the use and abuse of nature in contemporary India*, London 1995.

60. See for example the special issue of *Environmental Ethics*, 8, 4 (1986), 'Asian Traditions as a Conceptual Resource for Environmental Ethics', and J. Baird Callicott and Roger T. Ames (eds.), *Nature in Asian Traditions of Thought: Essays in Environmental Philosophy*, Albany, New York, 1989.

61. Michael Hechter, *Internal Colonialism: the Celtic Fringe in British National Development, 1536–1966*, London 1975.

Assurance and Anxiety: the Imperial Condition

THE pendulum – and mistaken perceptions of the pendulum – are, perhaps, too evident in history. And by history I mean both the manner in which humans have organised their economic, social, political and cultural lives in the past, interpreting the risks and opportunities around them, and the writing of history and historicist disciplines by modern scholars. As we have seen, Thomas Callander, in understandably veering from imperial apology to imperial anathema in his own lifetime, was illustrating the rapid shift from idealistic hope to anxious fear. In the twentieth century, we have swung exhilaratingly from the social concerns of the welfare state to the apparent ruthlessness of the free market, from closed and planned economies (like that of India) to a new openness, from protection to free trade, in eastern Europe from communism to hesitant capitalism, and in culture from the supposedly modernist monolith to post-modernist eclectic anarchy.

Yet another example of such a swing is the manner in which some commentators suggest that we have moved from a confident assertion of the progressive primacy of western technology to fears of its essentially destructive import. Thomas Richards, in his recent book, *The Imperial Archive*, contrasts the assertive, self-confident nineteenth century in western thought and action with the anxious, self-critical twentieth.[1] Yet this characterisation is not entirely convincing: the technical developments of the twentieth century have been on a scale unimaginable in the nineteenth. We have been either bemused or enthralled by the information revolution, with its superhighways and world wide webs, satellite surveillance and communication, 'Desert Storm' with its smart weaponry, not to mention medical and pharmacological 'advances' which suggest to some that it will not be long before our grandchildren will be living to 150. It may be that more are chilled than thrilled by these developments, but any reading of the propaganda suggests a continuing and powerful projection of a bold assurance in the technical achievements of the developed world.[2]

Moreover, the doom-laden visionaries of the environmental apocalypse no longer hold the field to themselves. As well as J. E. Lovelock's notion of Gaia, the self-correcting mother world, there is now a vigorous school of thinkers, it must be said largely adherents of the new right and the free market, who see the green doom as a modish expression of the left.[3] The effectiveness of Green politics, despite one or two apparent successes in recent times, has also come in for severe criticism both from within and without the movement. What's more Whiggism, with its belief in the progress, if not the perfectibility, of humans, simply will not lie down and die. Some of the practitioners of the new historicism in English and comparative literature take such a severely moralistic view of the past that they inevitably sell themselves as the apostles of a more acceptable future. Even in the field of race and culture, one of their most notable practitioners, Edward Said, has recently written that

> ... although the animosities and inequities still exist from which my interest in Orientalism as a cultural and political phenomenon began, there is now at least a general acceptance that these represent not an eternal order but a historical experience whose end, or at least partial abatement, may be at hand.[4]

Reading this kind of alleged radicalism, I am always tempted to shout out that warning of Edward Thompson, no mean radical himself, that we should not view the past 'with the massive condescension of the present'. We should perhaps remind ourselves instead that historical periods are invariably deeply ambivalent. Nowhere is this more true, and less expected, than in the imperial experience. To return to Edward Said, he has often been accused of occidentalising the West, reducing it to its caricatured essences in the same way that he criticises western orientalists for creating an essential and prefabricated Orient.[5] He and many of his followers use the word imperialism as a monolithic system of thought, the prerogative of self-assured imperialists sweeping all before them, even pursuing a coherent and consistent set of policies.

Nowhere is this perhaps more true than in the alleged imperial response to the environment. It would be tempting to see all the fretful studies of the environmental effects of imperialism, which I laid out in my first lecture, as modern phenomena contrasting strikingly with the overwhelming assurance of the imperialists themselves. But that would be a one-dimensional view. Imperial rulers and experts seem to have been in turn bolstered by over-weening confidence and wracked by debilitating doubt. The propaganda may offer a more selective vision, but as we shall see, intimations of disaster can be found in the writings of imperial rulers and their experts. It is true that they tended to externalise causation in order to exonerate themselves, but in identifying and predicting major species extinctions, in worrying about climatic and topographical change, in fulminating (and that is not too strong a word) about the loss of forests everywhere, and in condemning the land use practices of many peoples, mainly in-digenous, they are as much the originators of the millenarian vision as they are the villains of their modern counterparts.

The rest of this lecture will be divided into three parts. First, I shall examine the conviction of imperial commentators that it was part of their mission to dominate and enhance the environment and that they had the capacity to do so. Second, I shall review the manner in which this could nonetheless be combined with a powerful presentiment of developing threat. Third, the interaction of these two will be analysed through the formulation of policy within the context of notable political and cultural constraints. Throughout, I shall attempt to show that the conservation icon is not as pure as it is sometimes depicted, that the neo-Whiggish identification of developing sensibilities and progressively enlightened environmental policies does not necessarily fit the imperial case.

IMPERIAL RULERS AND THEIR EXPERTS: ASSURANCE

It was of course the powerful sense of scientific ferment of the late eighteenth and nineteenth centuries, interacting with technological change and political and military advance, which helped to convince Europeans that they had created for themselves a hitherto unrivalled opportunity to control nature. This was to remain a characteristic of not only the precursors and the practitioners of imperial rule, but more importantly, the propaganda associated with them from the early nineteenth to the mid-twentieth centuries. Although the new palaeontology and, above all, the publications of Darwin, were to stimulate the greatest debate of the age in respect of perceived conflicts between science and religion, there were many institutional sources for the European sense of acquiring unique insights and power. The work of individual observers was greatly enhanced by the founding of the whole sequence of scientific and cultural societies, as well as botanic gardens, not only in Britain but also in many parts of the growing Empire. These created what was in effect an archive to develop and, as some thought, complete the taxonomising of the world, confidently reducing flora, fauna, palaeontology, entomology and geology into carefully classified relationships trapped within their Latin trinomials and the pages of books and journals. Human societies continued of course to be subjected to the same process, though they were categorised in different ways.

As Mary Louise Pratt has argued in her book, *Imperial Eyes*, these developments turned almost all European travellers into scientific classifiers of one sort or another.[6] A growing sense of superiority was buffed up by the assumption that they alone had both the interest and the knowledge to be able to do this. It also led to amateur polymathy on a generous scale. Nothing reflects this better than the activities of figures like the East India Company judge, Sir William Jones, and his associates in the Asiatick Society of Bengal, founded in 1784. Jones, it has been said, had a passion for codification and set about the ambitious task of effectively reducing the Orient to a complete digest.[7] What is so interesting about this society is that it effortlessly combined literary, religious and philological interests with those of natural history in all its forms. It is notable that an entire school of Scottish orientalists, products of their own Enlightenment, became associated with all this activity.[8]

Africa, of course, was viewed as a very different geographical and cultural context in which to pursue this work, but a whole series of travellers had embarked on major journeys of natural history exploration from the 1770s. The international character of this activity is neatly reflected by those who travelled inland from the Cape. These included the Swedes Thunberg and Sparrman, the Frenchman Le Vaillant, the celebrated Englishman John Barrow of Ulverston, later so powerful at the Admiralty and in the Royal Geographical Society, and the German Lichtenstein. Mungo Park in West Africa was more interested in the human societies among whom he travelled, but he also concerned himself with observations on fisheries, the wild and domestic animals of the desert, 'vegetable productions' (as he called them), ivory and elephant hunting.[9] These early examples could be multiplied many times.

Missionaries, of course, were never behindhand in these researches. Robert Moffat, who settled at Kuruman beyond the Cape frontier in 1821, published his *Missionary Labours and Scenes in Southern Africa* in the early 1840s.[10] This book is not only full of natural observations, but also represents an intriguing tension between some of the science of the day, which Moffat actually footnotes, and his inclination to view the landscape in religious terms: it was, he thought, a landscape that could be made to work

for Christians, but which obstinately served up drought and erosion
for the heathen, tree-cutting Africans.[11] Towards the end of the
book, there is an engraving of the mission, with ordered hedges,
paths, plantings and buildings contrasting with the wildness beyond.[12]

Moffat's son-in-law David Livingstone echoed this by suggest-
ing that one of the problems of the African was that he lacked a
'correct notion of the controul [sic] he exercises over the affairs
of the world'.[13] If we can translate 'affairs of the world' into
'nature', then we can sense Livingstone's own sense of a God-given
capacity to exercise a quasi-divine control. As a product of the
central belt of Scotland, Livingstone had good reason to share an
entire constellation of environmental ideas with many of the other
explorers, missionaries, traders, administrators, military men and
settlers who spread around the world under the umbrella of British
power. This mindset was made up of images of enclosure, draining,
improved farming practices and selective breeding in British agriculture, new approaches to hydrology through the constructive
application of water to transport and energy creation, the wider
application of fossil fuels – not just coal, but the oil produced by
his friend 'Paraffin' Young – and, of course, a particular obsession
of his, the almost redemptive power of steam technology. He was
well aware of the sense of command over landscape that had
emerged from the eighteenth century, together with the transformation of attitudes through those artistic expressions of control,
the sublime and the picturesque, which had been swept up into
the Romantic movement with its close affinities with geology.[14]

Settlers in the empire expressed this same sense of command
in practical, less cerebral ways. One early nineteenth-century
traveller in Ontario remarked that 'a Canadian settler hates a tree,
regards it as his natural enemy, something to be destroyed, eradi-
cated, annihilated by all and every means'.[15] As illustrations of
early settlements indicate, the wilderness, represented by that
untamed tree, was to be 'replaced by the cultivated and geometrical
order of the domesticated world'.[16] That Canadian settler spoke

for settlers everywhere. I suppose it was a similar sense of confident control that inspired that unfortunate man, Thomas Austin, a farmer near Geelong in Victoria, who has gone down in history as the introducer of the rabbit to Australia. He looked forward to some shooting for the pot, but unleashed countless millions of that major faunal pest on the entire continent of Australia. When Captain Cook deposited the pig in New Zealand, or again when sportsmen and domesticators introduced trout to the streams of Kashmir or the New Zealand southern Alps, where red and other deer were also let loose, they all imagined that the world was a place they could improve for the sake of both nutrition and sport. After all, in the nineteenth century they were only following the precedent of Scotland, where both landscape and fauna were controlled to enhance sporting opportunities, as in many places it continues to be today.[17]

What I find striking is the longevity of that sense of self-confidence. It can be found in the countless works of imperial administrators and propagandists as well as in the popular media down to at least the middle of the twentieth century. In one of his earliest letters home from Natal, even that hard-headed man of business Cecil Rhodes considered that Africa was so full of 'curiosities' that he ought to set about making a collection of them. Much later, his home at Groote Schuur beneath Table Mountain became something of a private botanical garden and zoo; he also gave many items, some of them looted from the future Zimbabwe, to the Cape Town Museum.[18] The earliest commissioners and governors of East and Central Africa in the Partition period were largely frontier freebooters with stronger interests in natural science than administrative techniques. Sir Harry Johnston, whom I shall return to later in the lecture, Sir Frederick Jackson and Sir Robert Coryndon were all in this mould. When Mary Kingsley set off on her first journey to West Africa she took equipment with her to collect and preserve reptiles, fish and insects. Her *West African Studies* contained natural history appendices with contributions by professional scholars.[19] To shift the geographical focus briefly to the Middle East and to the twentieth century, Sir Arnold Wilson, political officer in Persia and later British Commissioner in Iraq, declared in his memoirs that 'The voluminous notes from which this book has been compiled contain much historical and archaeological, geographical, geological, zoological and botanical information', which, together with 'meteorological, linguistic and ethnological data ... crowded the pages of my notebooks'.[20]

These examples could be multiplied many times, but here is a classic expression of this sense of control over nature. Sir Charles Eliot, Commissioner of the East Africa Protectorate, suggested in a book published in 1905 that the past of Africa had been uneventful and gloomy. This was due to the lack of contact with the outside world which resulted from natural obstacles, deserts, marshes, or jungles which separated the coast from the interior. 'The other continents', he went on, 'were once covered with forests and marshes, which have disappeared under the hand of man.'[21] Thus dramatic environmental change was the route to civilisation.

It was also the means to escaping environmental determinism:

Nations and races derive their characteristics largely from their surroundings, but, on the other hand, man reclaims, disciplines and trains nature. The surface of Europe, Asia and North America has submitted to this influence and discipline, but it has still to be applied to large parts of South America and Africa. Marshes must be drained, forests skilfully thinned, rivers be taught to run in ordered course and not to afflict the land with drought or flood at their caprice; a way must be made across deserts and jungles, war must be waged against fevers and other diseases whose physical causes are now mostly known.

It is a fascinating statement. Having smartly slid from environmental determinism to ecological control, he applies the language of discipline and training to nature in the same way that it was sometimes used for indigenous peoples who were cast in the role of children to be acculturated to the modern world. He writes of the caprices and barriers of nature that can be ordered by European skills. And he expresses the medical self-confidence that clearly arose from Ronald Ross's final exposure of the causes of malaria. In a final peroration he asserted that 'this contest with the powers of Nature seems a nobler and more profitable struggle than the international quarrels which waste the brain and blood of Europe and Asia'. Thomas Callander would have read that with considerable approval!

Eliot also included an ecstatic chapter on the Uganda railway and its capacity to tame British East Africa. In this he echoed many other exponents of the natural power of railway lines. The journalist G. W. Steevens, for example, described Kitchener's railway into the Sudan as 'the deadliest weapon' the British were forging against both the Khalifa and the desert that lay between them.[22] A similar pride in technical power can be identified in the purple prose of the Viceroy Curzon's speeches at the opening of great Indian railway bridges, in the fascination with engineers and technology of Kipling, in those two great lion statues that stood guard at the end of the Ganges Canal, and in the harnessing of the mighty Nile by the first Assuan Dam of Sir William Willcocks.

Almost fifty years after Eliot's book, the same sense of unlimited opportunity is still being projected. In a radio programme about the Empire transmitted in 1947, the groundnut scheme in Tanganyika was described as 'solid ground for hope, hundreds of miles of jungle cleared by science and the bulldozer with a real promise of a better life for African and European'.[23] Science and the steam engine of the nineteenth century had become science and the bulldozer in the twentieth. Despite the notorious failure of that scheme, rapturous language continued to be used of developments such as the building of the Kariba Dam on the Zambezi and the formation of the vast Lake Kariba in the 1950s, a time when people and animals could still be viewed as only minor obstacles to science and engineering, moved out of the way of the advancing waters with scarcely a minimum of protest.

The continuing thread that runs through this propaganda, even if it becomes less apparent in the actual practice, is the sense of unlimited opportunity that Africa and other parts of the Empire presented. Livingstone had hoped for peaceful cotton fields; others had written of minerals and foraged products like rubber. The official reports of the East and Central Africa protectorates in the 1890s, so often seen as a time of real environmental problems, are replete with such hopes. Sir Arthur Hardinge reported that Africa 'from the Zambesi to the Sahara' was more or less stuffed full of rubber 'and there seems no reason why there should be any falling off in the steadiness of the supply' for many years to come.[24] Just as the forests of the Indian Empire had been viewed as virtually inexhaustible in the early nineteenth century, so too did observers consider that African forests had well-nigh limitless potential. Few imperial explorers and officers were more alert to natural history than Sir Harry Johnston, yet he wrote ecstatically of the vast forests of the Mau Escarpment, Nandi Plateau and the slopes of Mt Elgon of the modern Kenya. He suggested that the mere thinning of these, which was actually necessary to their improvement, would provide millions of cubic feet of timber which would find a ready market in East Africa and beyond.[25]

Of course such officials were justifying their presence, lulling their Foreign Office and Colonial Office masters into imagining that the development of these territories would be worthwhile, ultimately productive even to the extent of fiscal self-sufficiency. But Sir Harry Johnston repays further attention, for he represents not just natural historical passions and the talking-up of the potential of empire in Africa, but also the sounding of notes of alarm. These are very evident in his campaigns to save African game and in his autobiography, published in 1923.[26]

IMPERIAL RULERS AND THEIR EXPERTS: ANXIETY

Johnston had trained as an artist and had spent many hours in his youth drawing and painting animals at the London zoo, learning of their anatomy by helping in their dissection. Johnston's first visit to sub-Saharan Africa had been in 1882, when he joined a hunting expedition of the Earl of Mayo to Angola as its natural history collector. In 1883 he conducted his own natural history expedition to Mount Kilimanjaro, sponsored by the Royal Society and the British Association for the Advancement of Science, a journey which, in common with similar French and German activities, had distinctly political overtones. When he duly became Commissioner of the British Central Africa Protectorate (now Malawi) and later of the Uganda Protectorate, he always insisted on being accompanied by his own natural history collector, a gentleman with the delightfully appropriate name of Doggett. He established botanic gardens and small zoos at his official residences in Zomba, Malawi and Entebbe, Uganda, and he published books which are full of his natural history researches and his own illustrations of animals, insects and plants, as well as the economic, ethnic and political potential of the territories.[27]

Johnston, like so many other natural history enthusiasts and hunters in the period, was particularly anxious about the decline of animals. When he had visited Tunisia in the late 1870s, he had found it still full of big game. When he returned as Consul-General in Tunis in the 1890s, the game had already disappeared. He joined the Society for the Preservation of the Wild Fauna of the Empire when it was founded in 1903 and was active in its demands for stricter controls upon hunting, particularly African hunting. But more interestingly, he has an almost throwaway line in his autobiography about Tanganyika. When he visited the Nyasa-Tanganyika plateau in what is now south-western Tanzania in 1890 he described excellent crops, a profusion of wildflowers and an abundance of game. By the early 1920s he was writing, 'The Tanganyika in those days was a paradise; later it was to be ravaged by wars, depopulated by sleeping sickness and afflicted in many other ways'.[28]

He was of course hinting that this crisis was partly, if not entirely, the product of German rule. Both in his treaty-making

on the foothills of Kilimanjaro and in the Cape-to-Cairo dream
which he shared with Cecil Rhodes he would dearly have
liked to keep the Germans out. Nevertheless, he was offering a
fascinating pre-echo of Kjekshus, whose work I mentioned in the
first lecture. But Johnston was far from alone and far from being
the first to note the environmental problems accompanying
imperial rule – accompanying, note, not necessarily resulting
from it.

Europeans were observing and worrying about the disappear-
ance of forests from at least the seventeenth century.[29] Scientific
contemporaries noted that deforestation produced multiple climatic and other environmental results, even if their warnings were
seldom heeded. From the late seventeenth century, observers of
ecological decline on oceanic islands – where changes were both
more rapid and more observable – became convinced that increasing desiccation was human-induced. By the early nineteenth,
many botanists and foresters were sure that deforestation led to
declining rainfall and a combination of droughts and flash floods
when rain did fall. This obviously produced soil erosion, the silting
of rivers and in some places desertification.

In India, from at least the 1840s, medical botanists who enjoyed
high prestige as members of the Indian Medical Service – and
many of them graduates of this University – started to warn of
the need for the preservation of forests, the setting up of a forest
department, and the extension of state control into foreign con-
servancy. Hugh Cleghorn, from Fife and an Aberdeen graduate,
became known as the 'father of the Indian forests'.[30] E. P. Stebbing,
a distinguished Indian forester at the turn of the nineteenth and
twentieth centuries, later Professor of Forestry at Edinburgh, wrote
a series of monumental works charting both the development of
the Indian forest service and the growing crisis which made it
necessary.[31] He devoted entire chapters, incidentally, to quantifying
the insatiable fuel demands of British Indian towns and cities. In
the 1930s, while still occupying his chair, he also visited West
Africa to study forestry there in all its aspects, including the onward

march of the Sahara.[32] He argued that the alarming denudation of tree and bush cover resulted from the damaging effects of indigenous pastoralism and shifting cultivation.

In both India and Africa, the pinning of the blame for environmental degradation on indigenous peoples was an almost universal imperial phenomenon. For imperial rulers, triumph and tragedy seemed to follow hard on each other's heels. As we saw in the first lecture, it has been suggested that even those grand achievements of imperial hydrology, the canals of North-West and South India, began to go sour. Literally so, for they had led to salination and waterlogging and may well have stimulated the spread of tropical malaria.[33] Faced with this failure, imperial officials often accused the users of misuse or inadequate maintenance. Similarly, indigenous land use was indicted as the main source of degradation. The use of fire by hunters and gatherers, pastoralists and agriculturalists was everywhere condemned. As we have seen with Stebbing in West Africa, nomadic pastoralists, in particular, were universally accused of damaging grasses beyond repair and destroying bush cover and woodland through the fires they lit to encourage fresh growth.[34] Shifting or swidden cultivation in all its forms, now often seen as a sensible response to fragile ecologies, received its full share of disapproval in India, Africa and elsewhere.[35] Forest dwellers who had interacted with woodlands for countless centuries were seen as highly damaging to the trees Europeans now wished to conserve.

This condemnation of the alleged destructiveness of indigenous peoples was nowhere more apparent, and perhaps more debatable, than in the case of hunting. At the end of the nineteenth century, Europeans became convinced of the vast reduction in wild animal stocks in many parts of the world, but particularly in Africa. From the early years of the century down to the 1870s, Africa was often portrayed as a natural Eden, teeming with wildlife and full of plant and animal species waiting for the collector and classifier. William Cornwallis Harris, an East India Company officer who travelled into the interior from the Cape to shoot in the 1830s, described a 'perfect panorama of game', including one scene in which he counted 300 elephants as well as countless other animals. He had, incidentally, been encouraged to head inland by Andrew Smith, a doctor, naturalist and hunter and an Edinburgh graduate.[36] He was succeeded by a much more colourful and violent Scot, Roualeyn Gordon Cumming, from Altyre in Morayshire, who claimed to have hunted in southern Africa in the 1840s in his kilt and 'Badenoch brogues', and there are engravings in his book that seem to prove it!

Cumming saw 'plains teeming with game', a 'hunter's elysium', 'a never-ending succession of every species of noble game'. His reaction to this was to indulge in 'hecatombs of slaughter'. He eventually became a showman at home, exhibiting his trophies and publishing books that contain countless harrowing descriptions of animal deaths, including those of his own horses, oxen and dogs. Forty-five horses and seventy dogs died of disease or were killed coursing antelope, bringing elephants to bay and chasing lions.[37] Cumming's celebrated book, which made him the 'lion of the season' (as his *Dictionary of National Biography* entry quips) when it was published in two volumes in 1850, casts a very curious light on Keith Thomas's enlightened Romantic sensitivities. Neither Cumming's tastes nor his technology led him to consider the virtues of the clean kill. On one occasion he refrained from killing a sable antelope he had wounded until he had tested his dogs on the blood spoor. His use of dogs and their frequent deaths in confrontations with lion and elephant indicate that he made little distinction between the wild and the tame which some have seen as the significant criterion of animal sensibilities. Once, when he had disabled an elephant, he kindled a fire and put on the kettle to prepare coffee. 'There I sat in my forest home', he wrote, 'coolly sipping coffee with one of the finest elephants in Africa awaiting my pleasure behind a neighbouring tree.'[38] His descriptions of the death throes of animals are invariably harrowing. Once he gave an elephant thirty-five musket balls and waited for him to halt and die:

At length he reduced his pace to a very slow walk; blood flowed
from his trunk and all his wounds, leaving the ground behind him
a mass of gore; his frame shuddered violently, his mouth opened
and shut, his lips quivered, his eyes filled with tears.[39]

At length, the gratified Nimrod watched his prey rock forwards
and backwards and then fall over in death. The influential animal
philosopher Mary Midgley has used these and similar passages to
suggest that they do indeed imply sensitivities, arguing that Cumming illustrates 'a true belief in the consciousness, complexity and
independence of the victim'.[40] She goes on to propose that this
apparent cruelty towards elephants is not necessarily analogous to
callousness towards people. I am afraid that I find her work, in this
regard at any rate, as wrong-headed as her inability to spell Cumming's name properly. She simply reveals a totally inadequate
understanding of the vast range of nineteenth-century hunting literature or its relationship to descriptions of military campaigns
against African peoples at the turn of the nineteenth and twentieth
centuries.

At any rate, Harris and Cumming were but the precursors of
an extraordinary number of elephant hunters, hunters for skin
and horn, including both Boers and British, who travelled
deeper into the interior of Africa, pushing forward the game
frontier as they went. The Boer hunter, Jan Viljoen, described
how all forms of game had swarmed in areas of the western
Transvaal in the 1840s, but by the 1860s had been almost com-
pletely wiped out. Many of the larger game, he averred, could
now only be found north of the Limpopo.[41] In 1860, a massive
game drive was laid on in the Orange Free State for the visiting son of Queen Victoria, Prince Alfred, later Duke of
Edinburgh. Some 25,000 head of game had been enclosed and
driven by hundreds of Africans. Over 6000 head of large game
were allegedly shot, together with many more speared by Africans
and Europeans, and there were several African fatalities caused by
the charge of a terrified herd of Burchell's zebra.[42] One of the

prince's companions, Major General Bisset, described the mode
of hunting:

> The Prince fired as fast as guns could be handed to him, for Currie
> rode on one side and I on the other, and we alternately handed
> guns to him as he discharged his own ... It became very exciting
> to see great beasts larger then horses rolling over from right and
> left shots ...' [43]

Another account described animals as worn out in their exertions
to escape, standing about scarcely seeking to evade their destroyers.
Sir George Grey, the Governor, lost his dignity and gravity and
the ladies struggled to join in.[44] Meanwhile, 'the sportsmen looked
more like butchers than sportsmen, from being so covered with
blood. His Royal Highness and Currie were red up to the
shoulders from using the spear'.[45] By the 1890s no game could
be seen on the same plains at all.

In my book, *The Empire of Nature*, I argued that game formed
a significant subsidy to the whole processes of imperial advance.[46] Although David Livingstone, strikingly and unusually for
his age, expressed some anxieties about the slaughter of game, he
still permitted his early journeys to be subsidised from ivory sales.[47]
Tusks and rhinoceros horn financed many expeditions in Africa,
as well as mineral prospecting, the establishment of mission stations
and the operations of companies like the African Lakes and the
Imperial British East Africa. Troops, porters, workers at missions,
towns, farms and the building of railway lines were all fed on
game. White settlers securing large tracts of land (standard farm
sizes in Mashonaland were 6,000 acres, in Matabeleland 12,000)
were often able to survive initially by asset-stripping game (as well
as woodland). Meanwhile, the pachyderm frontier proceeded
further into the interior of the continent. Selous had difficulties
hunting ivory in the 1870s and 1880s because elephant had
retreated into the tsetse fly country and across the Zambezi.

By the 1890s, imperial officials and sportsmen (sometimes one
and the same) were trumpeting the decline and potential fall of

large African mammals, particularly the pachyderms: many thought that elephants and rhinoceros were ripe for imminent extinction. While they occasionally blamed the profligate European hunter with his devastatingly accurate high-velocity rifle, generally they held Africans to be responsible. Several decades earlier, David Livingstone saw the problem as resulting from the wider availability of firearms: 'as guns are introduced among the tribes all these fine animals melt away like snow in spring'.[48] Later Selous complained that one trader in Matabeleland had supplied 400 Ndebele with guns to shoot game, so that its products could be exported.[49] Elephant hunters in the upper Zambezi in what is now Zambia similarly used auxiliary African hunters.[50] Soon the Society for the Preservation of the Wild Fauna of the Empire was lamenting the 'appalling' 'destruction of game throughout the British Empire, and particularly in Africa'.[51] One member of the society, reflecting a common view of the time, suggested that securing meat by hunting was the stamp of primitiveness. Meat should be obtained from domestic animals and hunting should be reserved for sport.[52]

It was this contrast between the symbolic and in many respects quasi-medieval dominance of the landscape through the chase and the humble utilitarian needs of people living within it that came to be enshrined in the hunting law of the period. From the 1890s and particularly after the signing of a Convention for the Preservation of Wild Animals, Birds and Fish in Africa in London in 1900, these laws were internationalised. The use of the word 'preservation' is significant since it had always been applied to preserving game for sport on European estates. It has a quite different ring from the word 'conservation' that was coined later.

The developing conviction that the decline in African game resulted from African subsistence hunting, together with hunting for export stimulated by European traders and gun providers, led colonial authorities to erect a mighty hedge of legislation which was designed to exclude indigenous hunting, to restrict the hunt to European officers, settlers and travellers who could afford hunting licences and comply with the regulations which indicated that only shooting with modern rifles was permissible.[53] African techniques of traps, snares and nets, hunting with dogs, spears or arrows were all banned. They no longer complied with a sporting code which insisted on an ideal of the clean kill, preferably of older male animals, effected by the lone European sportsman with his advanced high-velocity rifle. Such a code had been impossible in the days of the musket and it figures barely at all in the works of Harris, Cumming and others. It was an invention of the late nineteenth century affected, it seems to me, not so much by developing sensibilities as by improving technology and the transfer of the class relationships of land ruler, land owner, sportsman and poacher to Africa. Much the same sort of regulations had already been introduced into India and Ceylon, where the native shikaris (hunters) became a dying breed by the end of the century.

However, the concept of the 'penitent butcher' seems to me to be an unconvincing one. Conservation was an economic, social and class phenomenon in which the very sensitivities the neo-Whigs claim to identify were used as arguments for the framing of legislation. The activities of Cumming and the Duke of Edinburgh just a few decades earlier either indicate an astonishingly rapid conversion or proof that it is dangerous to lay too much store upon gradually developing sensibilities which somehow prove a unique humanitarianism on the part of the West. Thus while Europeans were recognising some of the environmental problems that accompanied the establishment or extension of their rule, they were sufficiently convinced of the power of the new science and the new technology to carry all before them that they externalised the responsibility for ecological degradation. But they went further than this: fearing their own apocalypse in tropical and sub-tropical territories where the rate of change or the depths of the climatic and environmental cycles were so much more pronounced than in temperate zones, they resorted to dramatic palliatives. What seemed like extreme problems stimulated extreme solutions.

IMPERIAL RESPONSE TO
ENVIRONMENTAL CRISIS

To understand the character of this reaction to perceived environmental change, it is helpful to turn to imperial mapping of colonial territories. A good deal has been written about the significance of maps in both representing an iconography of power and in supplying the knowledge through which it could be extended and maintained.[54] What is often missed, I think, is the manner in which the neat delineations of maps supplied an imperative to policy. When imperial cartographers drew lines on maps, whether lines of communication or lines of land use, they were seeking to create simple, comprehensible and clearly demarcated systems. Specialist land use seemed to fit scientific rigour. It created blocs that could be administered and policed in appropriate ways. A settler territory like Southern Rhodesia (Zimbabwe), for example, came to be divided up into a whole series of different land specialisms: land occupied by or purchasable by settlers, African reserves, African purchase land, game reserves, Crown land either for alienation to whites or to be maintained as wilderness, as well as cities, towns and transport corridors. Similar divisions, with varying categories, could be found in India, the white dominions, and other African territories, particularly those with white settlers.

Of course these zones could never be pure: both whites and indigenes lived in cities, even if the theory was that the latter were there on a temporary basis, while whites needed native labour on their farms. But separation and 'purity' were the ideal. Thus, the notion of indigenous people living within a game reserve or national park, and co-existing with animals, was considered to be unacceptable. Not only might they be tempted to be 'poachers', it would be an additional burden on park staff to police them and supply the administrative functions that were properly offered in 'native' reserves. Sometimes the medical imperatives of sleeping sickness supplied an excuse for moving such dispersed people and concentrating them in larger, more readily observed and administered villages. Transhumant pastoralists were a particular problem. States tend to feel uneasy about people they cannot pin down and post-colonial states have been equally anxious in this respect. So efforts – and it should be stressed that they were efforts, often fruitless – to settle nomads and similarly separate them from lands demarcated for other purposes, whether settler purchase, animal conservation or forests, proceeded apace.

Moreover, the colonial commercial imperative – empire existed for trade and revenues depended on it – led to pressures upon indigenous farmers to produce export cash rather than food crops. Government agronomists set out to teach African peasants to specialise rather more in mono-cultivation as well as introduce the European ideal of 'clean agriculture'. This meant avoiding the African practice of intercropping standing cereals with ground crops like squash or pumpkins and promoting the cutting down of trees which cultivators often left standing, for good reasons, in their fields.[55] In addition, officials and anthropologists became convinced that pastoralists concentrated more on quantity than quality in farming their herds.[56] Drought and erosion led to compulsory destocking on a massive scale in many colonies.

In India, forests since time immemorial had been the homes of the so-called aboriginal tribes who practised to varying degrees a combination of swidden agriculture, pastoralism and hunting.[57] Other peasants, both in India and in Africa, operated on the margins of the forest, sometimes clearing for agriculture, sometimes pasturing animals in forest glades, exploiting forest products and hunting. Often the forest, like the hunting of animals in many places, offered a hedge against famine in times of drought. For forest officers, people were anathema. Forest services everywhere inveighed against what they saw as the wasteful and destructive depredations of forest dwellers. They could only feel comfortable that a forest was a genuinely protected zone when the humans had either been excluded or placed under tight controls. A forest should be a wilderness, a great empire of nature as one Indian forest officer put it, where foresters could not only pursue their work of research and protection against the day of beneficial exploitation but hunt at will for recreation. E. P. Stebbing's literary output included not only his works of forest history and policy, but also several books of Indian shikar.[58] The two went together, as inseparably as did the viceroy and his howdah on a tiger shoot, or official hunts in India and Ceylon, which were often seen as significant points of contact between British rulers and indigenous princes.

When blocs of land are being set out in this way, the structure and iconography of the map demand that they should appear to be significant. The protected forests of India, surrounded by a wealth of forest legislation, covered 21% of the land area of the sub-continent. In East, Central and southern Africa, game reserves, later translated into national parks, took up vast tracts of territory, in several instances amounting to 10% or more of the land area of the colony. Almost all of these, like the celebrated parks of Kenya and Uganda, the Selous in Tanganyika, the Kafue and Luangwa in Northern Rhodesia, the Matopos and others in Southern Rhodesia, the Kruger in the Transvaal involved the dispossession and removal of local peoples. Anyone who has visited the Matopos hills can testify to their eerie emptiness, and this a region well populated until the 1890s. If you predict an apocalypse too assiduously, and react too dramatically, you can end up with a planned apocalypse.

To change continents, it is now well-known that the preserved wilderness that was the ideal of the Dunbar-born John Muir in the western United States was, like so many nineteenth-century 'traditions', an invented wilderness. National parks in Canada and New Zealand also involved the dispossession of native peoples.[59] The creation of the first park in the Canadian Rockies in the 1880s had a great deal more to do with the commercial interests of the Canadian Pacific Railway than with conservation. The Stoney Indians were removed from the region of the hot springs around Sulphur Mountain and Banff, and it became instead a playground of a white elite travelling the CPR rails. In New Zealand the three mountains, Ruapehu, Tongariro and Ngauru-huo were handed over to the Government in 1887 by a Maori chief who was trying to protect his people and their holy places from the encroachments of a rival Maori group and white graziers. It was fully protected as a national park in 1894 by the celebrated New Zealand minister of lands, John McKenzie, born in Kintail. This and other New Zealand national parks, particularly in the South Island, became the setting for the acclimatisation of dozens of species of mammals, birds and fish from Europe and elsewhere.

Millenarian environmental prophecy is of course a weapon with which to beat authorities into action. But the predicted apocalypse often leads to the planned apocalypse. The setting aside of vast tracts of land for forest and game reserve, the efforts to create specialist land use, to settle nomads, consolidate shifting cultivators and clean up 'primitive' agricultural practice created their own ecological crises. Moreover, the terror of the advancing tsetse fly, producing nagana in cattle and trypanosomiasis or sleeping sickness in humans, also led to extremes of policy, the massive culling of game in southern Africa, the often disastrous concentration of villages, leaving empty bush as a haven for the tsetse to expand in East Africa.[60] The pendulum had swung too far.

But there is always a gap between intention and effect, a gulf often between expert analysis and executive action. And there is an even more significant chasm between policy and practice. What may seem like good intentions are often resisted on the ground or alternatively can produce wholly unintended outcomes. In my third lecture, I shall be looking at indigenous environmental knowledge and the capacity it sometimes offered for resistance. How far did imperial policies actually work and to what extent have they been abandoned or maintained in more recent times? I shall also be feeding in the Scottish dimension. Was there a distinctive role for Scots in all this and is there any evidence for a reciprocal influence upon Scotland itself?

NOTES TO LECTURE TWO

1. Thomas Richards, *The Imperial Archive: Knowledge and the Fantasy of Empire*, London 1993.

2. J. E. Lovelock, *Gaia: a new look at life on earth*, Oxford 1979; *The Ages of Gaia: a biography of our living planet*, Oxford 1988.

3. Such figures include Wilfred Beckerman, Matt Ridley and Richard D. North. See, for example, Richard North's *Life on a Modern Planet*, Manchester 1995; John Vidal, 'Apocalypse Never', *The Guardian*, March 16 1995.

4. Edward Said, 'East isn't East: the impending end of the age of Orientalism', *Times Literary Supplement*, 3 February 1995. See also his 'Afterword' to a new impression of *Orientalism*, Harmondsworth 1995.

5. John M. MacKenzie, *Orientalism: History, Theory and the Arts*, Manchester 1995, p. 13.

6. Mary Louise Pratt, *Imperial Eyes: Travel Writing and Transculturation*, London 1992.

7. Edward Said, *Orientalism*, Harmondsworth, 1985, p. 78. See also Garland Cannon, *The Life and Mind of Oriental Jones*, Cambridge 1990.

8. Jane Rendall, 'Scottish Orientalism: from Robertson to James Mill', *The Historical Journal*, 25 (1982), pp. 43–69.

9. Mungo Park, *Travels in the Interior Districts of Africa: performed under the direction and patronage of the African Association in the years 1795, 1796, and 1797*, London 1799, chapters XX and XXIII.

10. Robert Moffat, *Misssionary Labours and Scenes in Southern Africa*, London 1846 (first edition 1842).

11. Moffat, *Missionary Labours*, p. 87. See also Grove, *Green Imperialism*, p. 71.

12. Moffat, *Missionary Labours*, p. 147.

13. Quoted in Angus Calder, 'Livingstone, Self-Help and Scotland', in John M. MacKenzie (ed.), *David Livingstone and the Victorian Encounter with Africa*, London 1996, p. 90.

14. From a vast literature, see for example Christopher Thacker, *The Wildness Pleases*, London 1983. The Lake poets were of course closely connected with the great geologist Adam Sedgwick.

15. Anna Jameson, *Winter Studies and Summer Rambles in Canada*, Toronto 1938, quoted in Brian S. Osborne, 'The iconography of

nationhood in Canadian art', in Denis Cosgrove and Stephen Daniels, *The Iconography of Landscape*, Cambridge 1988, p. 165.

16. *Ibid.*, and see the illustration of the residence of D. Y. Williams, J. P., Hiller Township, Ontario, also p. 165.

17. Quoted in Robert I. Rotberg, *The Founder: Cecil Rhodes and the Pursuit of Power*, New York 1988, p. 40.

18. *Ibid.*, pp. 387, 389.

19. Mary Kingsley, *Travels in West Africa*, London 1897, pp. 692–733.

20. Sir Arnold Wilson, *S. W. Persia, Letters and Diary of a Young Political Officer, 1907–1914*, London 1942, pp. vi–vii.

21. Sir Charles Eliot, *The East Africa Protectorate*, London 1905, p. 4.

22. G. W. Steevens, *With Kitchener to Khartum*, Edinburgh 1898, p. 22.

23. Quoted in John M. MacKenzie, '"In Touch with the Infinite", the BBC and the Empire 1923–53', in John M. MacKenzie (ed.), *Imperialism and Popular Culture*, Manchester 1986, p. 183.

24. Sir Arthur Hardinge, *Report on the Condition and Progress of the East Africa Protectorate from its establishment to the 20th July 1897*, C 8683 (1897), p. 48.

25. Quoted in David Anderson, 'Managing the Forest', in Anderson and Grove, *Conservation in Africa*, pp. 251–2.

26. Sir Harry H. Johnston, *The Story of My Life*, London 1923.

27. See for example Sir Harry Johnston, *The Uganda Protectorate*, London 1902.

28. Johnston, *Story of My Life*, p. 276.

29. Grove, *Green Imperialism*, chapter 3.

30. E. P. Stebbing, *Forests of India*, 2 vols, London 1922, vol. 1, p. xiii. See also Grove, *Green Imperialism*, pp. 451–3.

31. E. P. Stebbing, *Forests of India; Jungle By-Ways in India*, London 1911; *The Diary of a Sportsman-Naturalist*, London 1920.

32. E. P. Stebbing, *The Forests of West Africa and the Sahara*, Edinburgh 1937.

33. Elizabeth Whitcombe, 'The Environmental Costs of Irrigation in British India: Waterlogging, Salinity and Malaria', in Arnold and Guha, *Nature, Culture, Imperialism*, pp. 237–59.

34. Stebbing, *Forests of West Africa*, pp. 1–2: shifting cultivation, in Stebbing's view, was 'the most primitive form of agriculture known to man'. He felt (*ibid.*, p. 5) that forest degradation occurred in three phases: 'farm it, graze it, then hunt it'.

35. The British banned 'bewar', one of the Indian forms of shifting cultivation, in the forest areas. Ramachandra Guha, 'Prehistory of Indian Environmentalism: intellectual traditions', *Economic and*

Political Weekly, January 4–11, 1992, pp. 57–64. See also Ramachandra Guha, *The Unquiet Woods: Ecological Change and Peasant Resistance in the Himalaya*, Delhi 1989; Jacques Pouchepadass, 'British Attitudes Towards Shifting Cultivation in Colonial South India: a Case Study of South Canara District 1800–1920', in Arnold and Guha (eds.), *Nature, Culture, Imperialism*, pp.123–51, and for Africa see the article by Millington in Anderson and Grove (eds.), *Conservation in Africa*.

36. William Cornwallis Harris, *The Wild Sports of Southern Africa*, London 1839; MacKenzie, *Empire of Nature*, pp. 94–6.

37. Roualeyn Gordon Cumming, *Five Years of a Hunter's Life in the far Interior of South Africa*, 2 vols, London 1850; MacKenzie, *Empire of Nature*, pp. 96–100.

38. Cumming, *Five Years*, vol. II, p. 92.

39. *Ibid.*, p. 63.

40. Mary Midgley, *Animals and Why they Matter*, Athens, Georgia, 1984, pp. 14–16.

41. Quoted in Andrew A. Anderson, *Twenty-Five Years in a Wagon: Sport and Travel in South Africa*, Cape Town 1974 (first edition 1887), p. 300.

42. John A. Pringle, *The Conservationists and the Killers: the Story of Game Protection and the Wildlife Society of Southern Africa*, Cape Town 1982 has an account of this hunt on pp. 39–43 and points out that despite the fact that the Prince was only sixteen years of age, there was no public outcry at the slaughter of game.

43. Major General J. J. Bisset, *Sport and War or Reflections of Fighting and Hunting in South Africa from the Years 1834 to 1867 with a narrative of HRH the Duke of Edinburgh's Visit to the Cape*, London 1875, p. 195.

44. *The Progress of HRH Prince Alfred Ernest Albert through the Cape Colony, British Kaffraria, the Orange Free State, and Port Natal in the Year 1860*, Cape Town 1861, pp. 88–9.

45. Bisset, *Sport and War*, p. 197.

46. MacKenzie, *Empire of Nature*, pp. 116–17 and *passim*. See also John M. MacKenzie, 'Chivalry, social Darwinism and ritualised killing: the hunting ethos in Central Africa up to 1914', in Anderson and Grove (eds.), *Conservation in Africa*, pp. 41–61.

47. David Livingstone, *Missionary Travels in South Africa*, London 1857, pp. 486, 562–3; W. Edward Oswell, *William Cotton Oswell, Hunter and Explorer*, 2 vols, London 1900, vol. II, p. 20.

48. Livingstone, *Missionary Travels*, p. 152.

49. F. C. Selous, *African Nature Notes and Reminiscences*, London 1908, pp. 188–9.

50. MacKenzie, *Empire of Nature*, pp. 123–4.

51. Quoted in *ibid.*, p. 211.

52. *Journal of the Society for the Preservation of the Fauna of the Empire*, XII (1930), p. 56.

53. For a survey of game laws, see MacKenzie, *Empire of Nature*, pp. 201–11 and 217–22.

54. J. B. Harley, 'Maps, knowledge and power', in Cosgrove and Daniels, *Iconography of Landscape*, pp. 277–312. Harley's arguments have stimulated considerable controversy. See also Jeffrey C. Stone, *A Short History of the Cartography of Africa*, Lewiston 1995; R. Prabharkar and Madhev Gadgil, 'Maps as Markers of Ecological Change: a Case Study of the Nilgiri Hills of Southern India', in Arnold and Guha (eds.), *Nature, Culture, Imperialism*, pp. 152–84.

55. For example, the inter-war years of the twentieth century witnessed a particularly acute tension between African traditional agriculture and European agronomists in Southern Rhodesia (Zimbabwe). Some of the issues were still very much alive when I conducted field work in 'tribal trust lands' in UDI-Rhodesia in the early 1970s. The confidence (or perhaps arrogance?) of imperial science ensured that ethno-botany was a largely neglected field. It continues to need a great deal of attention.

56. Katherine Homewood and W. A. Rodgers, 'Pastoralism, conservation and the overgrazing controversy', in Anderson and Grove (eds.), *Conservation in Africa*, pp. 111–28.

57. Gadgil and Guha, *This Fissured Land;* Damodaram, 'Famine in a Forest Tract', *Environment and History*, 1, 2 (995), pp. 129–58.

58. As well as those cited in note 31 above, Stebbing also wrote *Stalks in the Himalayas: Jottings of a Sportsman-Naturalist*, London 1912.

59. John M. MacKenzie, 'Conservation in the Commonwealth: Origins and Controversies', in Richard Maltby and Peter Quartermaine (eds.), *The Commonwealth, a Common Culture? Essays by Shridath S. Ramphal and others*, Exeter 1989, pp. 63–77.

60. MacKenzie, *Empire of Nature*, chapter 9; 'Experts and Amateurs', in MacKenzie, *Imperialism and the Natural World;* Ford, *Role of Trypanosomiases.*

The Imperial Sceptic

NEWS of the death of the world, or parts of it, has often been exaggerated. In 1968 Paul Ehrlich predicted massive famines on a global scale with millions starving to death. While there have been serious famines in Africa in the intervening period, war and political incompetence have been as much responsible as environmental degradation. In the late 1960s, a Club of Rome book forecast imminent eco-catastrophe, with pollutants, including car-induced smog, killing large numbers of people. Fears of continuing population growth in India led to mass sterilisation policies in the 1970s. In 1985 a senior World Bank official announced at a development conference that 'Africa is on the brink of ecological collapse'.[1] The image of Africa projected by the media is often selective and sad, but the continent is still very far from a total environmental catastrophe. These predictions of imminent disaster have duly taken their place among a long historic litany of such prophecies, few if any of which have so far come to pass. Alarmist calculations of risk are always intended as stimulants to policy. The threat that achieves the ideal combination of plausibility and fear is the one that is best likely to secure the most extreme policy reaction. As I suggested in my last lecture, even imperial confidence was balanced by its own doom-mongering. And conviction in scientific advance and technological power led imperial experts and rulers to believe that they could plan and control the environment. But as economics has taught us, all forms of planning can be frustrated by the fears and expectations, resistance and inefficiencies of people acting individually and as groups. We can now see that imperial planners failed to ride the tiger of environmental change, perhaps exacerbating as much as they ameliorated the ecological crises they themselves had partially stimulated. They thought they controlled events in nature but in truth, nature usually controlled them.

I strongly suspect that scholars in the twentieth century (and this is still true of the discourse theorists and new historicists in literary studies) have been taken in by imperialists' estimation of their own power. Perhaps one of the contributions of environmental history will be to emphasise the comparative weakness of imperial rule. To test this we need to look at the gap between policy inputs and practical outcomes. For the implementation of policy is a very inexact science, even in the imperial context. Imperial rule too often gives the impression of being an administrative paradise. It has been said that intellectuals gravitated to empire because they had the opportunity to test ideas without the trammels of domestic politics. An autocratic system facilitated both the framing and implementation of policies. It was easier to ride roughshod over indigenous peoples whose own interests and concerns could more readily be ignored than those of a metropolitan population. Empire was a domain for the expert, for experts found more receptive ears on imperial rulers than they ever found on politicians at home.[2]

Perhaps there is something in all this, at least in the realm of imperial self-perception, but in retrospect it is possible to see that the constraints of empire were as great as, if not greater than, those at home. The British system, unlike the French, was never centralised or uniform. It was complex and heterogeneous in the extreme. At any given moment, colonies of white settlement could be found on a constitutional spectrum from dependent territory, representative government, responsible government, dominion and federal status. India was a complete empire of its own, hugely diverse in the character of its presidency and provincial governments and, at various times, responsible for the imperial relationship with Burma, the Persian or Arabian Gulf, Aden, Zanzibar, Afghanistan and the semi-independent states of the

Himalayan foothills. The princely states, constituting a third of the land area of the sub-continent, varied from the vast Hyderabad to small principalities scarcely larger than a Scottish estate. In Africa, there were major policy differences between the West African colonies and those of East and Central Africa. Those in the South-Central area more or less fell into the orbit of white-dominated South Africa. This example illustrates the ways in which frontiers of influence ebb and flow, from Limpopo to Zambezi to Congo frontier, and back again. To all of these must be added the great assortment of Caribbean, oceanic and offshore islands with their own traditions – often longer standing – and colonial systems. Moreover, within imperial territories, there were often tensions and rivalries that could frustrate policies: for example between forest departments and those promoting commercial and private interests, between game and agricultural services, native administrations and the military or other agencies.

All of these colonial governments fell under at least three offices of state in Whitehall, the Foreign Office for protectorates, the India Office for India and its associated territories and the Colonial Office for the rest. The Dominions Office was added in the 1920s. The Admiralty, the Horse Guards and the War Office were also heavily implicated in all military and associated matters. Viceroys, Governors, High Commissioners and Residents came and went, each imposing a distinctive, whether effective or nor, stamp on his territory. Similarly, policies could come and go according to the predilections of successive and often politically alternating secretaries of state. In the dominions, the imperial authority be-came, in the words of Goldwin Smith, no more than 'a ventriloquial apparatus'. It is true that colonial circulars, proposing action sometimes on the basis of international consultation or conventions, were despatched around the empire. And instances of model legislation, not least in the areas of forestry and game protection, were passed from colony to colony, with Indian examples in the former very influential, but again imperfect ap-plication of the law must have been endemic. In any case, in all imperial territories the usual tensions between state power and private interest were abundantly apparent. In settler colonies, particularly in Africa, these tensions were exacerbated by the conflict not only among different sectional groups, but also with the interests of indigenous populations.

Indigenous peoples varied (on an economic scale) from hunters and gatherers to complex peasant and urban societies; and (on a political spectrum) from highly developed states to decentralised acephalous (literally 'headless') societies. The concept of indirect rule preserved – and in some cases enhanced – the power of these states and their traditional rulers. Elsewhere, states were quite simply invented to fit the people to the theory rather than the theory to the people. In some places (northern and north-western India for example) pastoral hillmen were viewed by the British as superior and 'manly' people, martial races suitable for recruitment as auxiliaries in the imperial army. (In concentrating on men, I merely reflect the contemporary bias.) In others pastoralists were seen as mobile destroyers to be pinned down and settled. By the later nineteenth century, the peoples of empire were also placed in a social Darwinian racial hierarchy and policies towards them were often modified according to their perceived place in such a scheme.

Much of this diversity is well known, if often misunderstood in practice. But less closely observed has been the heterogeneity of the imperial ruling group. This diversity can again be analysed ethnically, socially and functionally. In a status-conscious empire, particularly in India, those concerned with government, with commerce, with the military, missions and the professions held very different positions within a strictly hierarchical and snob-ridden imperial society. Moreover, not only were there French in Quebec, Dutch in South Africa and continental European émigrés and Jews everywhere, there were also fine distinctions among English, Scots, Welsh and Irish. It is the complexity of the imperial contribution by this ethnic mix from the United Kingdom which is, I think, the great hidden story of imperial rule. English historians of empire have always had a tendency to lump all together as British, blurring cultural distinctiveness in linguistic uniformity.

THE SCOTTISH CONTRIBUTION

Some Scottish commentators in the nineteenth and twentieth centuries, starting I suppose with Sir Walter Scott and on through John Hill Burton and W. J. Rattray to Andrew Dewar Gibb, sought to highlight the Scottish contribution to empire.[3] Gordon Donaldson wrote a pioneering book, *The Scots Overseas*, in 1966, though it dealt mainly with colonies of settlement.[4] The Anglo-Irish Ascendancy has sometimes been seen as the Junker class of empire, with the Royal Irish Constabulary as the prototype for imperial police forces (a view recently challenged).[5] Migration historians have necessarily disaggregated the ethnic components of settlement and in Canadian, Australian and New Zealand history there has been a lively debate about the Scots or other contribution to the cultural mix of those countries.[6] Recently, I published an article which argued that, although the administrations and legal systems of the British Empire were essentially English in form, the Scots succeeded in exporting some significant aspects of their distinctive civil society to the empire.[7]

In this analysis, I was following George Elder Davie's celebrated characterisation of the Union as the bipolar 'unification in politics, separation in ethics', that through her educational, intellectual and commercial/ financial traditions, Scotland made a distinctive 'cultural contribution to the world'.[8] There is a good deal of evidence to suggest that this is true. Eighteenth-century commentators, some admittedly from the standpoint of hostility, never ceased remarking on the overweening influence of the Scots in the East India Company. There was a remarkable group of such men around Warren Hastings, for example.[9] They seem to have gained privileged access to both company clerkships and regimental success.[10] By the beginning of the nineteenth century an entire school

of Scottish administrators had emerged in India, figures such as
John Malcolm, Thomas Munro and Mountstuart Elphinstone.[11]
Elsewhere, from the Montreal merchant houses to their equivalents
the 'hongs' of the Far East, from the agency houses of Calcutta
to the Australasian Loan and Investment Company, Scots busi-
nessmen, financiers and investors were strikingly dominant.[12]

When you read the works of imperial travellers, it is surprising
how high was the reputation of Scots. I am sure that this is because
they were written up as a distinct antidote to the writing down
of the Irish. Edward Long, whose *History of Jamaica* was published
in 1774, extolled the virtues of Scots as craftsmen and doctors in
the West Indies, while positively vilifying the Irish. Anthony
Trollope, touring the empire in 1873, noted that 'in the colonies
those that make money are generally Scotchmen, and those who
do not are mostly Irishmen'.[13] Certainly the Scots were viewed
around the empire as a means of keeping Popery at bay: Scots
ministers and their kirks were encouraged to emigrate for this very
purpose. Sir Charles Dilke, who travelled round the empire in
1867, remarked that 'wherever abroad you come across a Scotch-
man, you invariably find him prosperous and respected'. Indeed,
so dominant did Scots seem to Dilke that he considered it 'strange
indeed why Scotland has not become the popular name for the
United Kingdom'.[14] Froude, visiting Australia in 1885, came to
similar conclusions.[15] The great actor, Sir Henry Irving, remarked
in a speech in 1896 that 'he had an idea that when the North Pole
is eventually found, it will bear a strong resemblance to Arthur's
Seat'.[16] One observer remarked that 'I began to think that either
the world was very small or that Scotland was very large'.[17]

It was of course emigration that was very large, but this does not
entirely explain the predominance of the Scots in several significant
professions, and none more so than the medical. As early as 1731,
John Drummond of Quarrel, a Scots director of the East India
Company, wrote to his brother a testy letter on the subject:

I have told you once and again not to recommend any surgeons

to me, for all the East India Company ships have either Scots
Surgeons or Surgeon's mates, and till some of them die I can, nor
will, look out for no more, for I am made the jest of mankind,
plaguing all the Societys of England with Scots surgeons.[18]

By the beginning of the nineteenth century, it is a well-known
fact that graduates of this University dominated the medical service
of the East India Company. And doctors of course were also
natural scientists, botanists in particular. One of these Aberdeen
graduates, Dr. Charles Maclean, was celebrated for trying to
establish freedom of expression in India under the imperious rule
of the Marquis Wellesley.

These botanist doctors bring us firmly back to our main environmental track. James Anderson, Robert Kyd, William Roxburgh
and John Forbes Royle (though not all from Aberdeen) were
instrumental in developing the botanic gardens at Calcutta, Bombay
and Saharanpur. As John Hargreaves has pointed out, Aberdeen-
trained botanists dominated the Calcutta garden into the twentieth
century.[19] It was from the ranks of the botanist doctors that the
first foresters came, and they were more or less aware of forestry
and climatic ideas developed in Europe under the influence of
French botanists as well as the environmental theories of Alexander
von Humboldt. Hugh Cleghorn, Alexander Gibson, John Croumbie Brown, all Aberdeen graduates, are among the founders of
forestry science and colonial forest policy. When Brown gave
evidence to the 1866 parliamentary committee on the possibility
of establishing a national school of forestry, he stated that he
considered that 'Scotchmen can be most efficiently, and at the
least expense, trained up so as to manage our Colonial forests
advantageously. That is a particular point to which I have given
attention'.[20] As we have seen in earlier lectures, Scottish missionaries
like Moffat and Livingstone had a keen eye for natural historical
and environmental issues. As we well know, John Muir of Dunbar
is seen as one of the founders of American environmentalism.

Why this ethnic specialism? Why should Brown have placed

such emphasis on Scots' suitability for training in forestry? There is, perhaps, a whole range of explanations which we could probably debate for a considerable time. The obvious one is the distinctive academic fare of Scottish universities, particularly in this case in medical and botanical training, combined with a Calvinist predisposition to effect a relatively easy reconciliation between science and religion. It is well known that the work of the Rev. Thomas Dick helped David Livingstone to cease worrying about this great nineteenth-century conflict and both medicine and botany were of course well represented in the Aberdeen curriculum. Moreover, the Scottish Enlightenment helped to create institutional and personal connections with the botanical, natural historical and environmental ideas developing on the Continent. But we can go further. Scotland offered an extreme case of deforestation. Though not fully understood until the twentieth century, this helped to stimulate a considerable literature of hunting and natural history. Some Scottish landowners had begun major replanting schemes. And the kind of efforts at planning faunal resources, ranging from concepts of the noble and the huntable to vermin to be destroyed, if not exterminated, also became a model for imperial game policies. What is more, Scotland became a 'typical landscape' which was used as a touchstone for imperial travellers.

Mountainous landscape, with its distinctive hydrology and climate, as rediscovered through Romanticism and the concept of the sublime, came to be admired throughout the empire, as ironically did people who lived in mountains. Although the Highlands had been largely depopulated and their history partially expunged, nonetheless the perceived ethnicity and culture of Highlanders was artificially transferred to the whole country. Those of us who have endured those recent and wildly ahistorical films *Rob Roy* and *Braveheart* will know what alarming results this can have, even turning the impeccably Lowland Elderslie into a medieval Highland clachan. Nineteenth-century travellers, illustrators and painters seemed to need landscape referents to understand the exotic territories which they visited. Thus some of the earliest paintings of

Canada and Australia depict what can only be described as georgianised landscapes, looking suspiciously like parks laid out by Capability Brown. But mountains almost everywhere seem to have conjured up Scotland: whether it was the Shire Highlands in what is now Malawi, the Ceylon hill country, some of the gentler parts of the Himalayan foothills, or mountains and the equivalent of sea lochs in New Zealand and Canada, all produced this almost automatic comparison.

In the twentieth century, John Buchan continued this tradition, twisting the referential landscape into a sign of civilisation. Writing of Natal in his novel *Prester John*, Buchan's narrator and hero, David Crawfurd, proclaims:

> All of a sudden I realized that I had come out of savagery. The burden of the past days slipped from my shoulders. I felt young again, and cheerful and brave. Behind me was the black night, and the horrid secrets of darkness. Before me was my own country, for that loch and that bracken might have been on a Scotch moor.[21]

Moreover, Buchan beautifully represents the sporting interests of shooting, fishing and mountaineering which became the characteristic pursuits of officials and military throughout the empire wherever opportunity presented itself.[22] Just as an English elite used Scotland as a vast outdoor playground, so did the empire develop its characteristic wildernesses, sometimes fabricated wildernesses, in which those three sports could be pursued. Any trawl of the vast numbers of imperial memoirs reflects the manner in which aristocrats, the rich, the gubernatorial class, forestry officers and other officials with the opportunity pursued such activities both in the empire on short leaves and in Scotland when on longer leaves at home. A celebrated figure like Sir Samuel Baker combined the exploits of hunter in Ceylon, explorer and Nimrod in Africa, with notable forays against the stag in that centre of the Scottish hunting cult, Glen Tilt.[23] What is more, some of the most notable hunters of the nineteenth and twentieth centuries, from Gordon Cumming to Denis Lyell, were Scots.

Thus Scotland stood for wilderness, if a civilised, tamed and controlled wilderness. It offered a familiar model by which other wildernesses could be judged. By the twentieth century, Malcolm Fraser Darling was exposing both the human origins of that wilderness and the degree to which it represented environmental degradation, in his famous phrase, the 'wet desert'.[24] And he, fascinatingly, made comparisons with Africa in identifying the extent to which wilderness was self-inflicted by human resource use. There is, then, a tremendous complex of cultural, historical, environmental and educational reasons why Scots were seen as the ideal protagonists of environmental services within the empire.

IMPERIAL CONSTRAINTS AND LOCAL KNOWLEDGE

Tracing intellectual and cultural traditions is one thing, identifying their influence upon policy is quite another, particularly in the complex situation described above. Grove's *Green Imperialism* makes two rather unwarranted assumptions. The first is that if the ideas are there, then policy must almost inevitably follow. The second is that policies based upon developing environmental ideas are essentially progressive.[25] To be fair to him, he has noticed the problems with this in other publications.[26] But the relationship between observation and action is a good deal more complex then he often allows. It is not the pure application of environmental ideas that matters, but the manner of their application.

We are now able to put together this strongly Scottish mediation of environmental ideas with the development of imperial policies. Grove sees the instrumentality of desiccationist and climatic theory as being best identified in Indian forest policy and its transference to the Cape Colony and elsewhere. Despite their marginal origins, those Scottish botanist doctors had high prestige within the East India Company service. Hugh Cleghorn and Alexander Gibson were able to use this prestige to argue for the foundation of forest policies, first in Madras in 1858 and later on an all-India basis. In 1862, John Croumbie Brown, lecturer in botany at this university between 1853 and 1862, brought the same set of ideas to bear on the Cape Colony when he was appointed colonial botanist there.[27]

But the differences between reactions at the Cape and in India are highly instructive. Cleghorn and Gibson worked within an essentially autocratic system, where state power was little trammelled by legislative constraints, though private interests were capable of asserting themselves with help from the metropolis. Yet as Gadgil and Guha point out, there were considerable policy conflicts, particularly in respect of attitudes towards the indigenous inhabitants of the forests.[28] They suggest that there were at least three different approaches, two of which were more liberal about attempting to combine forestry with the survival of forest communities. But the more rigid annexationist policy became the norm. Moreover, forest policy was heavily influenced by commercial imperatives, leading for example to the usual preference of the forester for faster-growing trees than the finer, but slower-growing oak.[29] Thus state power and the imperative of the market overwhelmed any consideration of community interests. Moreover, international expertise was brought to bear through the employment of German foresters, such as J. G. Koenig, Sir Dietrich Brandis, Wilhelm Schlich and Berthold Ribbentrop. Brandis, Schlich and Ribbentrop were the first three inspectors-general of Indian forests between 1864 and 1900.[30] However tempting it would be to see these German foresters as the heralds of a less liberal forest policy, in fact Brandis was keener on finding a reconciliation between imperial forestry needs and the rights of forest dwellers than his British counterparts.[31]

At the Cape, Brown was the successor of the Austrian botanist Ludwig Pappe, but by the 1860s settler government ensured that considerable influence would be exerted by private, albeit conflicting, interests. Indeed, in 1866 the post of colonial botanist was wound up in a period of retrenchment and Brown was made redundant. He withdrew to Britain to issue forestry propaganda through a series of books and representations to official committees.[32] Once full responsible self-government was granted to the Cape in 1872,

settler interests became even more powerful. This contrast helps
to emphasise that imperial diversity of which I spoke earlier.

It is all too easy for historians to become obsessed with stated
policy, with the fine detail of legislation and with the reports of
administrators, game wardens or forest and agricultural officers.
These often strain towards ideal situations, the perfect outcome
that all policy hopes to achieve, but seldom does. We should
never forget that laws are indeed followed more in the breach
than in the observance, that in the environmental history of empire
we are often dealing with vast areas with small numbers of people
desperately attempting to police them. Furthermore, policies,
particularly when based on visions of an apocalypse, often produce
results vastly different from those intended.

In the realm of game control, both in preservation for the elite
hunter and in the later conservation of a more modern kind, there
is good evidence that the colonial authorities over-estimated threat,
over-compensated in the laying aside of lands for game, and
unleashed new and more destructive forces upon the environment.
In the late nineteenth and early twentieth centuries, naturalists
repeatedly under-estimated the capacity of relict populations,
which they thought were heading for extinction, to make
remarkable recoveries. After the rinderpest epidemic of the 1890s,
all the game affected, like buffalo and the larger antelopes, re-
appeared in vast herds by the First World War. Hippos, a valuable
source of food to pre-colonial and early colonial travellers,
recovered their numbers to such an extent that in some places,
Uganda for example, they caused monumental damage to grazing
and riverine ecologies. They also posed a considerable threat to
crops. Elephants, whose doom had been much prophesied in the
later decades of the nineteenth century, were capable of becoming
a major plague once more within a decade or two of being
protected.[33] We have seen similar effects in recent years, with
considerable over-populations in South Africa and Zimbabwe and
a striking recovery in Kenya.

Planning animal control was also subject to extraordinary

cultural shifts. Elephant, rhinoceros and hippopotamus were often designated as royal game and subjected to the strictest licensing controls. Other animals were classified as vermin to be killed at every opportunity, much like the oft-criticised faunal priorities of the Scottish shooting estate. In Kenya, so-called vermin were killed in vast numbers by African poisoners amusingly known as *borgias*.[34] In many places, even those noble metaphors for empire, the tiger in India and the lion in Africa, were viewed as vermin and were shot at every opportunity. Shooting tigers was of course one of the prime rituals of British rule in the sub-continent; it was also the best means for a local administrator to symbolise his role in protecting the people. Shooting lions in Africa had a similar resonance, and was also a marker of the manly courage of European officials, settlers and sportsmen alike. Fascinatingly, the lion's fortunes were transformed by the internal combustion engine. In the 1920s, the first cars began to find their way to African game parks. Lions showed no fear of them, accepting them as a natural feature of the landscape. The game warden James Stevenson-Hamilton in what became the Kruger National Park in the Transvaal discovered almost overnight that lions, instead of being dangerous vermin, became the prime tourist attraction. He stopped shooting and starting conserving them almost immediately.[35]

Game law looks fearsome on paper. It perfectly encapsulates attitudes, but it does not offer a good guide to actuality. There is plenty of evidence to suggest that enforcement was lax or, appropriately enough, a hit or miss affair. I noticed that a Union-Castle line *Guide to South and East Africa*, designed to offer guidance, in its own words, to 'tourists, sportsmen, invalids and settlers', seemed to be fairly dismissive of game laws. In its 1911–12 edition, it suggested that 'the extent of territory to be watched over is so enormous that the authorities are not able to do very much in remote districts. Considerable harm is still done by natives and others who are beyond the ken of the authorities'.[36] No doubt avid sportsmen were encouraged by such a remark, while still having the satisfaction of seeing blame pinned on Africans. There is also a good deal of evidence to suggest that very few cases were actually brought under the game laws. In the case of Kenya, enforcement was probably the lowest priority of the game department until the late 1930s. One white rogue hunter called John Taylor proudly boasted of his activities as a poacher and ivory exporter until at least the Second World War. The Game Department was astonished to discover in the 1950s that elephants were still being killed with poisoned arrows by specialist hunters from the Waata and Kamba peoples. Indeed, it may be that it was the counter-insurgency tactics learnt during the Mau Mau rising which helped in the inauguration of effective anti-poaching campaigns from the late 1950s.[37]

The re-discovery of poisoned arrow hunting by specialist elephant hunters as late as the 1950s is a salutary reminder that traditional knowledge and techniques can survive all manner of efforts to eradicate them. It also reminds us that, to secure a complete picture, we need more than the legislator's view from above. We also need the view from below. It is in this area that a good deal of recent work has concentrated. Many studies have demonstrated that the environmental knowledge of indigenous peoples can be highly refined in terms of their own strategies of survival, and such strategies can include significant contributions to conservation practice. It has been argued, controversially, that the environmental ideas of the new religions of Buddhism and Jainism were a response to some of the profligacy of early medieval India.[38] More securely, it does seem that different Indian castes established ecological niches for themselves, exploiting different aspects of their environment. Some hunting groups concentrated on different prey or left refuges for animals to recover their numbers. Small-scale tank irrigation was probably more ecologically friendly than later massive canal works. It has been suggested that the Mughal emperors avoided the taxation of forests and fisheries in order to encourage sustainability. We know that one people in South India carefully conserved a large bird population in order to supply guano as fertilizer for their agriculture. Fisher folk have long had techniques for preserving their stocks. Pearlers in the Pacific, Ceylon and the Arabian Gulf dived only in a specific season and on banks known to have regenerated their oyster stocks.[39]

Concepts of sustainable hunting were promoted by indigenous rulers in both India and Africa. The King of Nepal as early as the 1860s was an ardent preservationist, protecting forests in the Terai for economic exploitation and attempting, not very successfully, to restrict white hunting activities. A few decades later, the Maharajah of Kashmir, recognising the severe inroads on animal stocks made by the excessive popularity of tourist hunting, introduced conservation measures and divided up the hunting grounds into 'blocks' to be hunted and preserved in turn. Hunters in northern Uganda used a system of 'blocks' and strict territorial segregation to ensure that over-hunting was prevented. Lobengula, King of the Ndebele in south-western Zimbabwe from 1870–1893, created his own set of game rules and fined European hunters for infringing them. He also independently established the concept of 'royal game' for the species he regarded most at risk.[40]

There is also good evidence to demonstrate that in the nineteenth century Africans knew more about the complex ecological and physiological characteristics of the tsetse fly than Europeans did. With all their scientific pretensions, European travellers were often dependent on indigenous knowledge. In 1914, the Scots doctor Sir John Kirk, at the age of 81, gave evidence to the Colonial Office Sleeping Sickness Committee and insisted to his sceptical hearers that more than fifty years earlier he had noted that Africans knew the precise location of the fly, its relationship to nagana in cattle and to the game which acted as hosts to the trypanosomes. He also learnt from them that the warthog and bushpig were particularly important hosts of the fly as well as antelope and buffalo.[41] The hunters R. C. Cumming, Frank Vardon, William Cotton Oswell (the latter two travelling associates of David Livingstone) and Frederick Selous all testified to the importance and detail of African knowledge and advice.

Livingstone himself, who significantly placed a picture of the tsetse on the title page of his best seller *Missionary Travels and Researches in South Africa*, learnt a great deal from African observation and understanding of natural phenomena. King Lobengula was enabled to push cattle posts further into fly country as a result of elimination of game. The entomologist C. F. M. Swynnerton described in detail the techniques of the Gaza kingdom of Mozambique to control and separate game, tsetse and cattle. The Gaza king, Mzila, even established a game reserve known as the 'Oblong' where hunting and game drives were conducted.[42] Similarly, linguistic and other evidence suggests a wealth of knowledge of soil types, forest products and faunal characteristics in both Africa and India.

It should not be surprising then if we find that such peoples were sometimes capable of beating imperial administrators at their own game. There were major movements of peoples; game in certain areas was indeed shot out; tree cover was greatly reduced and soil degraded or eroded, particularly when people used to swidden agriculture or other forms of nomadism were settled; diseases did advance, sometimes as a result of wrong-headed environmental policies. But for some peoples it was perfectly possible to go on defying white policy and legislation. This was also true of white settlers, whose approach to ownership of ranching and plantation lands in Africa and India was one that made them a law unto themselves. There is increasing evidence to suggest that in Africa, outside the Union of South Africa at any rate, and possibly in some instances in India as well, it was not until the 1930s that forestry, game and police departments, together with agricultural services, were able to impose much stricter regulations on native peoples.

By that time, the anthropologist of Indian aboriginal tribes, Verrier Elwin, English in nationality but Calvinist in religion, had revealed the fate of people like the Baiga, the Agaria and the Gonds at the hands of the British forest authorities. The latter had almost succeeded in separating them from their traditional swidden agriculture, hunting and gathering, and charcoal-making in the forests. One of Elwin's Gond friends told him that his idea of paradise was 'miles and miles of forest, without any forest guards'. But still there was defiance. One Baiga told him that 'if the government passes a hundred [game] laws, we will do it. One of us will keep the official talking; the rest of us will go and shoot the deer'.[43] When conducting my research, I discovered a Pathan saying: 'First a white man comes to hunt animals; then two white men come to make a map; finally an army comes to conquer us. It is easier to shoot the hunter first'.

In Kenya, Dorobo and Tugen peoples succeeded in confounding British forestry administration in the Lembus forest, perhaps at the expense of conservation needs.[44] In Nigeria, forest policies were partly frustrated by the conflicts between the forest administration and the indirect rule authorities which were particularly powerful in that vast imperial territory.[45] In the Gold Coast and Sierra Leone, efforts were made to follow Indian practice in afforestation and soil conservation, but with little success. Moreover, towards the end of colonial rule the British were beginning to turn cherished ideas upside down, even attitudes to that long-standing bugbear, shifting cultivation. In 1948, the Agriculture Department of Sierra Leone, in a dramatic conversion, announced that swidden cultivation 'may be less a device of barbarism than a concession to the characteristics of a soil which needs long periods of recovery and regeneration'.[46] It is a perfect statement of the patronising orthodoxy of the past combined with a recognition and new respect for African knowledge in the present.

Thus we have complex patterns of policies which insofar as they worked at all did so only within the constraints of multifarious political, commercial and administrative pressures. In some places, they produced wholly unanticipated results, often creating more severe difficulties than they were designed to solve. In others, they were successfully resisted, generally through the passive resistance of those who simply went on as they were accustomed to do. As one forest officer told Verrier Elwin, 'Our laws are of such a kind that every villager breaks one forest law every day

of his life'.[47] Others who were dispossessed or criminalised by
forest law or by specialised land use came out into open rebellion.
Some environmental policies were quite consciously used as in-
struments of social control. And, as I have shown, it was only
perhaps at the end of the imperial period that departments were
sufficiently equipped with both the staff and adequate techniques
to make those controls real. Yet it was precisely at that time that
many imperial policies began to be discredited and, in some cases,
were turned on their heads.

Nevertheless, many remained to be adopted, and sometimes
even heightened, by post-colonial independent governments. And
it is perhaps in this context that we face that final problem which
has been a running theme of these lectures – did the colonial
period represent a major rupture in the human relationship with
the environment, or did it merely introduce certain qualitative
and quantitative changes to a history of exploitation and problems
of the natural cycle that have always rendered that relationship
problematic? There can be no question that the most significant
imperial transformations were the globalisation of resource extrac-
tion, the considerable enlargement and extension of state power,
the primacy of the market and international trade, and the introduction of strict concepts of the ownership of land and its bounty.

At first sight, those certainly seem to represent something
approaching revolutionary change. But as we have seen, neither
imperial economics nor colonial administration and policies were
ever monolithic. The absence of true centralisation, of a master
mind to the whole project, ensured highly diverse and complex
results wherever colonial rule was brought to bear. Moreover, if
we pose the counter-factual question, what would have happened
without imperial rule, if these processes had taken place largely
through informal systems in a situation of theoretical political
independence, it is highly likely, as perhaps parts of Latin America
indicate, that the results would have been little different. Indeed
it is even possible that the imposition of direct imperial controls
may sometimes have ameliorated the impact of the globalisation

of Karl Polanyi's Great Transformation as an unavoidable phase in human history.[48]

What is also apparent is that, so far as environmental history is concerned, it is all too easy to privilege the imperial period. As our perspective lengthens and research broadens, it is more obvious that we should place it in the broader historical context of both pre-colonial and post-colonial eras. And as we do so, we cannot help flattening out the high drama of the imperial impact, noticing new understanding of a greater depth of natural cycles together with environmental pressures in almost all periods of human activity. Moreover, the view from below indicates that we should avoid being taken in by the propaganda, the alarmist visions, and the perfect solutions of those arguing from above. For example, when the nineteenth- and early twentieth-century writers on Indian forests wrote anxiously of their devastation and argued for protective legislation, their evidence should be analysed not just in terms of their supposed environmental enlightenment, but also the considerable axes that they had to grind.

Indeed, our greater awareness of indigenous response and resistance, as well as knowledge and collaboration, helps to confirm the difficulty of seeing imperial rule either as an ideological monolith or as a supremely effective system. It is always dangerous to see those upon whom elites impose their policies as a passive and unresisting horde ripe for economic mugging and environmental rape. People resist in all sorts of ways – and in this context modes of collaboration can sometimes be a form of resistance – and as we have seen they sometimes find propagandist friends among those who have come to dominate them. In grappling with imperial rule, native peoples were sometimes scoring off enemies within and without their own societies. Sometimes environmental policies enabled elites to strengthen their power; sometimes they weakened them, producing social change throughout the society.

If all this can appear like complex shifting sands, we can at least be quite clear that the imperial experience proves that the human capacity for environmental prophecy remains highly rudimentary.

As I argued in my second lecture, visions of an environmental apocalypse can lead to equally destructive apocalyptic solutions. Environmental policies reveal the follies and fallacies, limitations and liabilities, as well as the attempted creative concerns of imperial rule. Imperial rulers too often used the evidence of their supposed scientific and technological sophistication to imagine that they commanded nature, whereas in reality they summoned up a host of environmental sorcerers' apprentices. As often as not they lacked the spells to reverse the effects they had almost unwittingly set in train.

Even if we avoid the comforting notion of a self-correcting mother earth, it is nonetheless apparent that nature, as in the rebuilding of animal stocks in Africa, has a capacity to recover – and sometimes recover to a dangerous point – much more rapidly than humans anticipate. If we can draw any lessons at all from the imperial environmental experience, I think they are the following. First, we should always beware of neo-Whiggish interpretations of environmental ideas. Environmentalism is not the icon it is often cracked up to be, but a critical cultural phenomenon like any other. Thus, just like economic planning, all environmental management tends to have its positive and negative effects. A second and related point is that we should be wary of notions of environmental heroes and villains. As is all too obvious in the rise and fall of the reputation of someone like John Muir, the heroic can be transformed all too readily into the villainous. Third, the Scottish contribution needs to be evaluated in this light: it was certainly distinctive and Scotland constituted a major bridge between empire and the scientific thought of the Enlightenment both at home and in Europe. But we have to remember that it embraced the violence of a Cumming as well as the environmental sensibilities of a Cleghorn or a Brown, sensibilities which in any case could lead to forests and wildernesses which excluded indigenous inhabitants who had been accustomed to finding their subsistence within them.

Fourth, we should beware of predictions of extreme threat.

They can lead to equally extreme and no less damaging responses. Fifth, local knowledge should never be underestimated: top-down policies have time-and-again shown themselves to be inadequate and the bottom-up perspective is always a necessary corrective. Nor should we demean people by viewing them as helpless victims of economic and environmental behaviour promoted by systems or elites. And finally, we should never drop our sceptical guard in identifying environmental propaganda and the public emotions it attempts to whip up. Both the Braer and the Brent Spar incidents offer ample proof of that.

I should like to conclude by honouring the memory of Thomas Callander who made these lectures possible. It would be tempting to follow the spirit of his revulsion from imperialism by guarding against complimenting the University on the contributions its graduates made to empire. But that would smack of the condescension of the present. The graduates who manned the Indian Medical Service, developed the botanic gardens and pressed for the conversion of their environmental ideas into policy were honest and able individuals who genuinely believed in the virtue of their labours and objectives. This University, in common with others in the nineteenth century, modified its curriculum to meet the needs of the Indian Civil Service to ensure that Scots were not disadvantaged in this important career opportunity overseas. It also contributed greatly, as John Hargreaves has pointed out, to the technical services of empire in the twentieth century, when that notorious colonial recruiter, Sir Ralph Furse, devoted his passion for public-school, Oxbridge-educated products primarily to the administrative rather than technical divisions of the imperial civil service. Aberdeen also produced many missionaries and doctors, among them some of the earliest women recruited for work in the empire. Rather than celebration, we desperately need research on the relationship between Glasgow and Edinburgh and empire, to complement those fine studies of Richard Symonds for Oxford and John Hargreaves for Aberdeen. Research students and retirees, please note.

Thank you, ladies and gentlemen, for listening to someone from a University, Lancaster, which still has 469 years to go to its quincentennial. It may be interesting, but not very profitable, to speculate what the human relationship with the environment will be like in 2464.

NOTES TO LECTURE THREE

1. *The Guardian*, March 16 1995; the World Bank official is quoted in Richard Bell, 'Conservation with a human face: conflict and reconciliation in African land use planning', in Anderson and Grove (eds.), *Conservation in Africa*, p. 79.

2. John McCracken, 'Experts and expertise in colonial Malawi', *African Affairs*, 81 (1982), pp. 101–16 and MacKenzie, 'Experts and amateurs', in MacKenzie (ed.), *Imperialism and the Natural World*.

3. Sir Walter Scott called India 'the Corn chest for Scotland where we poor gentry must send our youngest sons as we send black cattle to the south'. John Hill Burton, *The Scot Abroad*, 2 vols, London 1864; W. J. Rattray, *The Scot in British North America*, 4 vols, Edinburgh 1880; Andrew Dewar Gibb, *Scottish Empire*, London 1937.

4. Gordon Donaldson, *The Scots Overseas*, London 1966.

5. Keith Jeffery (ed.), *'An Irish Empire'*, Manchester 1996, introduction, pp. 10–11.

6. There is a large literature on Scots in the Empire, particularly the territories of settlement, but see for example the work of Eric Richards: 'Scotland and the Uses of the Atlantic Empire', in Bernard Bailyn and Philip D. Morgan (eds.), *Strangers within the Realm: Cultural Margins of the First British Empire*, Chapel Hill 1991; 'Scottish Australia 1788–1914', in *That Land of Exiles*, Edinburgh, National Library of Scotland, 1988; 'Australia and the Scottish Connection, 1788–1914', in R. A. Cage (ed.), *The Scots Abroad*, London 1985. Also Tom Brooking, '"Tam McCanny and Kitty Clydeside": The Scots in New Zealand', in Cage (ed.), *Scots Abroad*.

7. MacKenzie, 'On Scotland and the Empire'.

8. George Elder Davie, *The Democratic Intellect: Scotland and her Universities in the Nineteenth Century*, Edinburgh 1961, pp. v, xv.

9. John Riddy, 'Warren Hastings: Scotland's Benefactor', in Geoffrey Carnal and Colin Nicholson (eds.), *The Impeachment of Warren Hastings*, Edinburgh 1989, pp. 30–57.

10. George Kirk McGilvary, 'East India Patronage and the Political Management of Scotland, 1720–1774', unpublished Ph.D thesis, The Open University in Scotland, 1989; P. J. Marshall, *East India Company Fortunes: the British in Bengal in the Eighteenth Century*, Oxford 1976, pp. 12–13 and *passim*; G. J. Bryant, 'Scots in India in the Eighteenth Century, *Scottish Historical Review*, lxiv (1985), pp. 22–41.

11. Martha McLaren, 'Writing and Making History: Thomas Munro, John Malcolm and Mountstuart Elphinstone: Three Scotsmen in the History and Historiography of British India', unpublished Ph.D dissertation, Simon Fraser University, 1992 and 'From Analysis to Prescription: Scottish Concepts of Asian Despotism in Early Nineteenth-Century British India', *International History Review*, XV (1993), pp. 469–501.

12. MacKenzie, 'Scotland and the Empire', p. 724.

13. Anthony Trollope, *Australia*, London 1873, p. 420.

14. Sir Charles Wentworth Dilke, *Greater Britain*, London 1872, pp. 373–4, 533.

15. J. A. Froude, *Oceana or England and her Colonies*, London 1886, p. 116.

16. Speech of Sir Henry Irving at Pen and Pencil Club Banquet, Edinburgh 17 June 1896: the Papers of Henry Irving and Ellen Terry, Shakespeare Centre Library, Stratford-upon-Avon, box 11, item 31. I am grateful to Professor Jeffrey Richards for this reference.

17. David Macrae, *American Presents and Men I Have Met*, Glasgow 1908, quoted in Cage (ed.), *Scots Abroad*, p. 80.

18. McGilvary, 'East India Patronage', p. 204.

19. Hargreaves, *Academe and Empire*, p. 65.

20. John Croumbie Brown, *Management of Crown Forests at the Cape of Good Hope Under the Old Regime and the New*, Edinburgh 1887, p. iii.

21. John Buchan, *Prester John*, London 1950 (first published 1910), p. 206.

22. John Buchan, *Memory Hold the Door*, London 1940, chapter 1.

23. Sir Samuel Baker, *The Rifle and the Hound in Ceylon*, London 1884; *Eight Years' Wanderings in Ceylon*, London 1855; *The Albert Nyanza: Great Basin of the Nile*, London 1866; *Wild Beasts and their Ways*, 2 vols, London 1890–91.

24. For the Scottish landscape and hunting, see Willie Orr, *Deer Forests, Landlords and Crofters*, Edinburgh 1982. Fraser Darling's African analogy is mentioned in Smout, 'The Highlands and the Roots of

Green Consciousness', p. 240. See also *Fraser Darling in Africa: a Rhino in the Whistling Thorn*, edited and presented by John Morton Boyd, Edinburgh 1992.

25. Grove, *Green Imperialism, passim*.

26. See, for example, Richard Grove, 'Colonial Conservation, ecological hegemony and popular resistance: towards a global synthesis', in MacKenzie (ed.), *Imperialism and the Natural World*.

27. Brown, *Management of Crown Forests;* Richard Grove, 'Early Themes in African Conservation: the Cape in the early Nineteenth Century', in Anderson and Grove (eds.), *Conservation in Africa;* Richard Grove, 'Scottish Missionaries, Evangelical Discourses and the Origins of Conservation Thinking in Southern Africa 1820–1900', in *Journal of Southern African Studies,* 15, 2 (1989), pp. 163–87.

28. Gadgil and Guha, *This Fissured Land*, p. 124 ff.

29. *Ibid.*, p. 142.

30. Grove, *Green Imperialism*, pp. 376, 397, 459–60; Stebbing, *Forests of India*, pp. xiii, 242–3, 262–3; B. Ribbentrop, *Forestry in British India*, Calcutta 1899. More recently, the role of Brandis and German foresters in India has been surveyed in Indra Munshi Saldanha, 'Colonialism and Professionalism: a German Forester in India', *Environment and History*, 2 (1996), pp. 195–219. A list of Brandis' publications can be found on pp. 218–19.

31. Gadgil and Guha, *This Fissured Land*, p. 124. See also Ramachandra Guha, 'Forestry in British and post-British India: a historical analysis', *Economic and Political Weekly*, 1983, pp. 1882–96; 'Forestry and social protest in British Kumaon, 1893–1921', in Ranajit Guha (ed.), *Subaltern Studies* 4 (1985), pp. 54–101.

32. John Croumbie Brown, *The Hydrology of South Africa*, Edinburgh 1875; 'A British school of forestry, present position on the question', *Journal of Forestry and Estate Management*, April-May 1881, pp. 4–12; 'An Argument for the organisation of a British school of forestry', *Proceedings of the British Association for the Advancement of Science*, 1885, pp. 421–8; *Management of Crown Forests*. The question of the influence of the Empire upon British forestry practice and the founding of the Forestry Commission in 1919 is a subject yet to be studied: it would make a fascinating piece of research.

33. MacKenzie, *Empire of Nature*, p. 249 and *passim*.

34. E. I. Steinhart, 'Hunters, Poachers and Gamekeepers: Towards a Social History of hunting in Colonial Kenya', *Journal of African History*, 30 (1989), p. 257.

35. James Stevenson-Hamilton, *Our South African National Parks*, Cape

Town, 1940, pp. 7–9; *South African Eden*, London 1937, pp. 200, 232–3, 267. For an extremely interesting modern account of the history of the Kruger National Park and its significance to Afrikaner nationalism, see Jane Carruthers, *The Kruger National Park: a Social and Political History*, Pietermaritzburg 1995.

36. *Union-Castle Guide to South and East Africa, 1911–12*, p. 221.

37. Steinhart, 'Hunters, Poachers and Gamekeepers', pp. 252, 261–2.

38. Gadgil and Guha, *This Fissured Land*, p. 81. See also note 60, lecture 1, above.

39. See, for example, Gadgil and Guha, *This Fissured Land*, pp. 20–5, 95–102; David Hardiman, 'Small-Dam Systems of the Sahyadris' and Peter Reeves, 'Inland Waterways and Freshwater Fisheries: some issues of control, access and conservation in colonial India', both in Arnold and Guha (eds.), *Nature, Culture, Imperialism*; the conservation of pearl banks (together with all other aspects of the fisheries) is detailed in J. G. Lorimer, *Gazetteer of the Persian Gulf, Oman and Central Arabia*, Calcutta 1915, appendix C, p. 2242 ff. A useful account of the Ceylon fishery, and conservation measures, can be found in Leonard Wolf, *Growing: an Autobiography of the Years 1904–1911*, London 1961, pp. 86–98.

40. These and other examples of indigenous conservation are to be found in MacKenzie, *Empire of Nature* and 'Experts and Amateurs', in MacKenzie (ed.), *Imperialism and the Natural World*, pp. 191–4.

41. The evidence of Sir John Kirk, *Report of the Interdepartmental Committee on Sleeping Sickness*, Cd 7249 (1914).

42. C. F. M. Swynnerton, 'An examination of the tsetse problem in North Mossurise, Portuguese East Africa', *Bulletin of Entomological Research*, 11 (1921), p. 335.

43. Verrier Elwin, *The Baiga*, London 1939, p. 84, quoted in Guha, 'Prehistory of Indian Environmentalism', p. 61.

44. David Anderson, 'Managing the Forest', in Anderson and Grove (eds.), *Conservation in Africa*.

45. Olusegun Areola, 'The political reality of conservation in Nigeria', in Anderson and Grove (eds.), *Conservation in Africa*, pp. 281–3.

46. Quoted in Millington, 'Environmental Degradation in Sierra Leone', in Anderson and Grove (eds.), *Conservation in Africa*, p. 238.

47. Guha, 'Prehistory of Indian Environmentalism', p. 61.

48. Karl Polanyi, *The Great Transformation*, Boston, Mass. 1957 (first published 1944).

Index